THE FIRST
ONE HUNDRED
YEARS OF
UPSON
COUNTY
NEGRO HISTORY

COMMUNITY, RAILROAD, SLAVERY, EMANCIPATION
CELEBRATION, BUSINESS, SCHOOLS AND GOVERNMENT

JAMES MCGILL

authorHOUSE®

AuthorHouse™
1663 Liberty Drive
Bloomington, IN 47403
www.authorhouse.com
Phone: 1 (800) 839-8640

Published by AuthorHouse   12/20/2017

ISBN: 978-1-5462-1850-0 (sc)
ISBN: 978-1-5462-1849-4 (e)

Contents

The Thomaston-Upson County Community has produced some great black leaders whom God has given the gifts to make a difference in THE FIRST ONE HUNDRED YEARS OF NEGRO HISTORYIN UPSON COUNTY. As I researched the history of Upson County, my soul got excited about what God can do through a willing vessel. In this book my desire is to encourage the next generation to become available vessels so that God can use them to be difference makers in this changing world.

I wanted to write this book to show how great Upson County thrived in the early 1800s and 1900s by investing their time, talent, and money to make this community great.

Unfortunately, there are very scarce recordings of early Negro settlers in Upson County and few vital statistics are available. Many of these early accounts have either been lost are destroyed. However, by painstaking effort and frequent review as this work progressed, it is believed that this volume is as accurate as humanly possible.

This book is dedicated to my deceased mother, Mrs. Carolyn McGill-Holmes, my beautiful wife of 42 years, Linda Napier-McGill, and my lovely daughter, Kornisha McGill-Brown, who have been my greatest cheerleaders on this journey. -

Of course, I cannot fully express my appreciation for those who accepted proof reading assignments and offered much support. Those wonderful people are Dr. Audrey Napier -Matthews, Jeffery McGill, Jennifer Rogers-Sullivan, Penny Cliff, David Patterson, and the wonderful staff at the Thomaston-Upson County Archives. These people gave me feedback during the writing process.

INTRODUCTION

On December 9, 1822, a Georgia law passed creating Pike County (out of the western portion of original Monroe County) and Crawford County (out of the northwestern part of original Houston County) in the 1822 Treaty. The Old Alabama Road was first the dividing line, but on December 20, 1825, a small portion of the extreme northwest corner of Upson County ceded back to Pike County. This Georgia Law created Upson County, taking lands from both Pike County and Crawford County. All parts of Upson County lying north of Elkin Creek, running the north-west corner of said county, was added to, and became part of the county of Pike.

The Chattahoochee and Flint Rivers, running a generally parallel course, join the Chattahoochee in the southwest corner of the state where Florida, Alabama, and Georgia converged directly from Atlanta, Ga. The Chattahoochee and Flint Rivers flow into the Gulf of Mexico, at one time a Spanish sea, but to the south and east of the Chattahoochee- Flint system there is a watershed dividing the streams that flow into the Atlantic from those that go into the Gulf.

Earlier the waterfall on the Chattahoochee and Flint Rivers had been chosen by the Indians as important centers of tribal life. At the fall on the Chattahoochee and Flint, trading paths leading to the Creeks and the Cherokees converged. Goods were bartered, traded, or exchanged in Atlanta and were loaded for shipment in the Chattahoochee and Flint Rivers.

The Lower Creeks, who lived on the Chattahoochee and Flint River nearest to Georgia, were unusually friendlier and less under the influence of the mixed-breed Alexander McGillivray, than were the Upper Creeks. The mixed-breed women learned to spin and weave and cattle were raised. White missionaries, who brought Christianity and formal education to the Indians' mission school, began in a small way around 1800, with the Cherokees being much more interested in education than the Creeks.

Agent Benjamin Hawkins was one of the federal commissioners for the Creek Treaty of Colerain in 1796, and he became Southern Indians' agent soon thereafter, and in 1801 was appointed creek agent on the Flint River. He established his agency up and down the Flint River with a model farm, nursery for fruit trees, blacksmiths, and artisans, on a plantation of his own, worked by slaves. Hawkins sought to use the skill of planting fruits to induce the Creeks to adopt the white cluster.

Out spoken Rebecca Latimer Felton may have exaggerated when she, as common as blackberries, was only articulating the annoyance of antebellum white women who witnessed the evolution of a hardy new hybrid of Georgians. The slave, Amanda, was really the wife of prominent planter, David Dickerson, as well as the mother of his children, and after the Civil War she legally inherited part of his estate

During the time period of slavery in America, the white slave owners would have sex with their black female slaves, and the result often was children being born. Many slave owners did not help their mixed blooded mulatto children; they labeled these children black and let their black mothers raise them. These white looking children were considered slaves just like their mothers.

Agent Benjamin Hawkins urged the Indians to engage in agriculture individually, rather than following the old communal method, but he succeeded mainly with mixed-breeds and with the owned Negro slaves. Indians took to livestock raising because of the decline in wild game and because it was easier than growing field crops. Some raised small amounts of cotton, and some women-learned to spin and weave. The old hunting and trade economy was declining, but most Creeks adopted new ways slowly. The Creeks were broken people and no longer a threat to the whites. Change was essential. Some Creeks, especially the mix-breeds, took up individual farming, and entered into business partnerships.

Booker T. Washington popularized the idea of industrial education, which formed the basis of the curriculum in schools. Such programs encouraged students to take sewing, housekeeping, carpentry, blacksmith, and above all, agriculture. The idea fit in well with prevailing beliefs in thrifty hard work. Industrial education was encouraged in schools.

Georgia's industrial production increased rapidly too. At the local level women knitted and sewed much more, and many returned to the system of carding, spinning, and weaving to meet their families' basic needs.

Agent Benjamin Hawkins

LOGTOWN COMMUNITY

Logtown Community, near Tobler Creek, located in the southeastern section of Upson County was one of the first to be settled, and was once one of the wealthiest, most cultural areas in Upson County. Logtown road ran from the town of Yatesville to Highway 19 near Flint River.

Logtown Community was the main artery of travel through many plantations with their two story, rather elegant homes for this period. Logtown Community was a prosperous trading center and the home of many prominent Georgia families such as the Kendall, Cunningham, Respress, Birdsong, Atwater, and Hightower families. Large plantations operated on the outskirts of town, while wealthy slave-owning merchants and farmers lived in houses near the town square, and scores of hired slaves served the local businesses as stable boys, depot hands, laborers and tradesmen, and served the white families as domestic servants

The first cotton mill in Upson County, the Franklin Factory, was built on Tobler Creek in 1833. The factory was not a large factory. In 1835, a group of New Englanders arrived to manufacture textiles. George P. Swift arrived from New York and subsequently purchased Franklin Cotton Mills, which started with 1,500 spindles, making coarse yarn.

Profits from the small mill enable d Swift to build another mill, Waymanville Cotton Mill, named for his brother-in-law, William A. Wayman. The mill housed 600 spindles, 120 looms, and manufactured sheets and shirts. The business was very successful, and their products were known throughout markets for their quality. The company operated six mule wagon teams and delivered their goods throughout the southern states.

Good Cunningham was born in Buckingham County, Virginia, March 1797, and he came to Georgia before the War Between the States, settling in Upson County. He acquired much property, and at the beginning of the war, was one of the largest land-owners in the county, owing a number of slaves, and two large mills in the Logtown Community.

Thomaston and Barnesville Railroad Company

Upson County Railroad

Upson County roads were inadequate in the state without any navigable river. Thomaston's best hope to share in Georgia's prosperity was to have her own rail link to the nearest major railroad. The merchants of Upson County were a marked village serving a country richly blessed with fruitful farmland and plenty water powered sawmills. Railroads provided the chance to become a major trading town.

In November 1836, three white delegates from Upson County, Dr. Jeremiah Beal, a physician in Thomaston, Upson County Treasurer William Cobb, and Samuel S. Curte, owner of a 650-acrce plantation and twenty-five slaves joined 107 delegates from other Georgia counties to converse in Macon to devise a system of internal improvement of Georgia to connect Georgia with the Mississippi Valley.

On Friday, November 22, 1839, three years later, Thomas Goode, *representative* of Upson County in the House of Representatives, introduced a bill into the Georgia Legislature to establish the Thomaston and Barnesville Railroad Company for the purpose of building a railroad from Thomaston to some point on the Monroe Railroad, at or near Barnesville, Georgia in Lamar County.

December 13, 1839, a state charter for the Thomaston and Barnesville Railroad Company was essential to the success of any railroad company for two reasons. It established a corporation with liability, protecting the stockholders, in event of failure from losses beyond their capital investment. It gave the company the power of eminent domain to select and acquire a right of way through private land. Upson farmers, typical of other contemporary railroad investors, hoped to benefit from a rail road in numerous ways. They expected financial profit on their investment with cheaper freight rates for their agricultural production. They also hoped that the proximity of railroad service would increase the value of their land.

Even while the link on the Thomaston and Barnesville new charter was dying, events had already begun in the winter of 1839-1840 which would dampen Upson County's optimism and scatter the prosperity of the cotton belt. Beginning in the late 1839, cotton prices, which had been artificially supported since the panic of 1837, plummeted with disastrous consequences for planters and merchants. Banks failed, and the depression lasted for five years, until cotton price recovered in 1844.

Weatherly Close and Company, an interstate slave traders company, owned by John, Isaac, and Joseph A. (Doc) Weatherly, based out of Guilford County, North Carolina, began to purchase land in 1844, 1848, and 1850 from Upson county farmers along the Thomaston and Barnesville Railroad. In February 1855, two years before the Central Railroad Depot in Upson County the land across the street from the depot was bought from land owner, M. D. Johnson, by Weatherly Close and Company, an interstate slave Traders Company.

The new Central Railroad Depot was located in the Town at the Five Point intersection where Railroad Street (North Hightower Street) and Bethel Street touch. On Friday, October 30, 1857, in a joyous carnival atmosphere, Thomaston's population swelled to a crowd of three or four thousand merry members from surrounding counties to celebrate the opening of the Central Railroad Depot at the Five Point intersection.

Fittingly, many celebrants arrived by a special morning train from Barnesville, pulled by the Macon & Western's locomotive, C.J. McDonald. Mr. McDonald pulled a trainload of festival-goers on a free demonstration ride up and down the new line. A ball was held in the village that night with music by a Macon Band.

A Georgia Messenger's News reported that "the main purpose of the Thomaston and Barnesville Rail Road was to expand Thomaston's cotton market" but he noted that "very little cotton has been brought into Thomaston, for sale or shipment. It is anticipated that some 8 or 10,000 bales would pass over this new road this season, which will doubtlessly be increase the next season, then wished that the largest success for this enterprise."

TRANSIT SLAVE POPULATION

In the 1800's the population of Upson County rose to over 9,910, of whom 4,488 (49%) were slaves. Colored Town, populated with mostly transit slaves, grew to a population of 2,105 from 1,150 (55%). Almost one quarter of the county's slaves lived in the Colored Town, which was an area covering only eight percent of the county. Thomaston, the county seat, received a large share of the county funds to maintain and operate the Inferior Court and a building for the courthouse and jail. The courthouse and jail were the only two public buildings in the county. The courthouse and jail were managed by County's Ordinary (Probate Judge) William A. Cobb.

Sally Barkley, a slave who lived on William A. Cobb's home place on the outskirts of Colored Town, told about the patroller in an interview. According to the white interviewer, Mrs. Blakely said that "before a slave could leave the district it was necessary to obtain a pass. When a slave was caught out without a pass, there were men who were known as Patrollers' who appointed themselves, to punish the slaves"

In the 1846 February Term of the Upson Superior Court involving the case of Henry Garland, Jr. vs. Isaac Weatherly, it stated that Henry Garland, Jr. sued out an attachment for $595.00 against Isaac Weatherly, "who resides outside of this state" for damages indicating that on February 6, 1845, Garland purchased from Weatherly a certain Negro man named Tobe, about nineteen years of age for $595.00 cash, in return for which Weatherly gave a Bill of Sale, warranting Tobe soundness and good title, and attested by Robert Graham (local farmer, age 62).

Garland alleged that Tobe was fatally diseased with chronic inflammation of the stomach, and he also had chest and liver aliments. Tobe grew worse and died in July 1845. Garland had spent $75 on nursing, clothing, and physical fees.

Sheriff Alexander Pace levied the attachment on "two Negroes: Lizzy and her child Catherine" on December 27, 1845, and summoned Robert Graham as garnishee. He also summoned Anderson Stafford and Joseph A. Weatherly as garnishees on December 30, 1845.

Guilford Speer, a slave, operated a business in town which accumulated wealth at two thousand dollars cash that exceeded the value of 45 percent of free households in the Georgia Militia District where he lived. Guilford Speer was born in 1808 and migrated into Upson County in 1827 as a slave of James Spier, a local merchant. Probably about 1830 after Jeff Cary's slaves had been moved to Upson County, Jeff Cary's slave, Ellen, married Guilford Speer. Guilford Speer began to accumulate modest capital in 1830 by working during the day as farmhand on James Spier's plantation and making shoes and other goods at night. By the late 1850, Guilford Speer operated his own harness and shoes shop in a prime location on the court house square. A house and a lot of land lying in the east back square of Thomaston in Upson County also belonged to Spier.

In 1818, Georgia Law had forbidden even free persons of color to buy slaves. Guilford Speer's purchase of his wife was the ownership of one slave by another, and was legally inconceivable. Jeff Cary's memorandum of sale discreetly left the buyers name blank. He owned merchants and farmers and lived in houses near the town square. Guilford Speer and Ellen lived in an apartment behind his shoes shop on the square which he rented from the County Sheriff Owens C. Sharman. A very few of the urban enslaved, usually craftsmen and their families, lived on town lots not shared with whites.

GENERAL JAMES WILSON'S MILITARY RAID THROUGH UPSON COUNTY

On January 1, 1863, the second executive order was issued by President Abraham Lincoln, named to specific states where it applied. The proclamation did not free any slaves of the <u>border states</u> (<u>Kentucky</u>, <u>Missouri</u>, <u>Maryland</u>, <u>Delaware</u>, and <u>West Virginia</u>), or any southern state (or part of a state) already under Union control. It had directly affected only those slaves who had already escaped to the Union side. After hearing of the Proclamation, more slaves quickly escaped to Union lines as the Army units moved south. The Union armies conquered the Confederacy, and thousands of slaves were freed each day until nearly all (approximately 4 million, according to the 1860 census) were freed by July 1865.

On January 9, 1865, the 13th amendment of the United State Constitution was passed at the end of the Civil War before the Southern states had been restored to the Union and should have easily passed the Congress. The 13th amendment of the United State Constitution stated that neither slavery nor involuntary servitude, except as a punishment for crime whereof the party shall have been duly convicted, shall exist within the United States, or any place subject to their jurisdiction.

The Congress shall have power to enforce this article by appropriate legislation. The amendment thirteen was enforced by Congress in early 1865, after the Civil War had ended, and many of the slave owners in Georgia were confused about by the thirteenth amendment censuring the slaves. The occupying soldiers of the U.S. Army soon published orders that clearly enforced President Lincoln's Emancipation Proclamation, which was proclaimed two and half years earlier".

Unaware of Lee's surrender on April 9 and the <u>assassination of President Lincoln</u> on April 14, General <u>James H. Wilson</u>'s <u>Raiders</u> continued their march through Alabama into Georgia. In early 1865, after the Civil War had ended, many of the slave owners in Georgia were confused about the status of their slaves.

On April 16, the <u>Battle of Columbus, Georgia</u> was fought. This battle is widely held to be the "last battle of the Civil War." Columbus fell to <u>Wilson's Raiders</u> about midnight on April 16, and most of its manufacturing capacity was destroyed on the 17th.

On April 19-20, 1865, with the Double Bridges in western Upson County secured, the victorious Yankees waited for other elements of Wilson's command to catch up before moving on to Thomaston, Georgia, a village of about 1,500 people.

The Thomaston Times in April 15, 1992 reported a historical article researched and written by David E. Patterson of Bartlett, Tennessee states:

"Sometime associated with Sherman's March to the sea through Georgia, Major General James Harrison Wilson's task was to destroy the agricultural and industrial facilities of the Deep South which had so far been untouched by the war. Columbus was captured after a fierce night's battle on April 16, 1865.

General Wilson ordered Lieutenant Colonel B. D. Pritchard to lead the Fourth Michigan and Third Ohio Calvary on a forced march to capture the Double Bridge. These were the two bridges which spanned either side of Owens's Island in the midst of Flint River just south of Sprewell Bluff, 10 miles west of Thomaston.

The spring weather was pleasant, but windy, and the roads were very dry and dusty. The invaders found the lands along their way previously untouched by the war; a rich country ripe for pillage and destruction. Families scrambled to hide foodstuffs and spoils anywhere including burying them in the fields. The first Federal Troops appeared and pandemonium reigned. Blacks cried, "Judgment Day has come."

Parties of soldiers entered houses and ransacked drawers, searched closets, and broke open trunks in search of something to steal, including family heirlooms, (something of special value handed down from one generation to another), which would never be seen again. Horses and mules were taken. Bales of cotton were set afire, stores of grain and bacon were ransacked, and mills were burned. Pillars of thick black smoke showed where three of Upson County cotton mills, including the Waymanville and Rogers Factories were burned. Federal Troops lit train cars on fire, and openly sent the flaming monster full speed toward Thomaston. The spectacular display of the fiery destruction, came to the end of the track and jumped the embankment near the City.

General Wilson's headquarters broke camp at 6:00 a.m. on April 18, 1865 to continue the brutal business of war. The buildings at the Upson County railroad depot in Thomaston and the Rock was put to the torch. General Wilson set out for Macon in a carriage confiscated with a team of horses from Mr. B.B. White of Thomaston. Eight days after hostilities ceased, while camped in Macon, Wilson ordered his officers to thoroughly search the persons and baggage of every enlisted man in his command to confiscate stolen property. The search produced enough gold, silver, jewelry, greenbacks and other plunder to fill an ambulance. Some men were found with five or six gold watches each and jewelry enough to open a store.

A great part of the people's store of feed had been taken to be destroyed. At least one Upson family raked up corn left by the horses at a Union Camped, washed and dried it, for something to eat. William Rogers, whose family fled as refugees to Wilcox County, later wrote, "I have often wondered how the people of Upson County lived the rest of the year." The Upson County Railroad, whose track, fortunately, had not been torn up, salvaged their locomotive and continued to operate in a crippled state until the end of 1865, when the poverty of the stockholders forced it to cease running.

WILLIAM GUILFORD THE FATHER OF THE EMANCIPATION CELEBRATION

In 1860, census suggested that several manufacturing businesses in Thomaston employed bonds people as skilled draftsmen and laborers. Guilford Speer and Emanuel Speer were among eight enslaved men who made boots, shoes, saddles, and harnesses in four different shops. Independent businessmen, William Guilford, Guilford Guilford, and Wallace Goods formed a co-partnership in a line of hair styling under Guilford Speer and Son's Barber Shop for the purpose of running a first class barber shop in 1873. They supplied good sharp razors, kept a clean shop, and did good work. The Guilford family opened the barber shop on downtown square across from the courthouse in Thomaston, Georgia where he and his family held a virtual monopoly of the barbering trade throughout the rest of the nineteenth century.

William Guilford adopted the Christian name of his father Speer Guilford as his own last name. William Guilford was born on the Hurricane Place Quarter. Victor Thurston credits William Guilford (former slave of the Spier and Birdsong families), with organizing the first Emancipation Celebration.

Williams Guilford was Upson County delegate to the Constitutional Convention of 1868, and Upson County Representative in the Georgia House of Representative in 1868-1870. William, a Republican, later served over a year as a legislator. William was one of many local home-grown Black activists of Reconstruction Georgia who numbered with leaders like Henry M. Turner and Jefferson Long, but who now usually languished in historical obscurity.

Although his political influence was almost entirely local to his home county, he founded a living legacy. William who was active in education for local freed people, was one of the founders and a prominent members of the St. Mary A.M.E. Church, where he organized a debating society, and participated in local political events. St. Mary AME Church had a new church building completed in1870 that provided ample room for scholars, and the school operated in St. Mary at least as late as 1876. Upson County did not open a public school in Thomaston for Negro students until August 1883; St. Mary can confidently claim credit for housing the first successful church school organized for the Negroes in Upson County.

William Guilford petitioned for homestead exemption for himself, his wife Lucinda age 33, and his four children Duffield age 15, Lucinda age 13, Douglas age 9 and Babe age 2, along with a detailed description of his possessions. In 1865 the Guilford Family was one of the most prominent families in Upson County.

In 1937, Victor Thurston (probably using oral history sources) wrote that forty days after General Wilson raided, on May 29, 1865, the slaves owners brought many of the slaves to the courthouse and announced to them that they had been freed. This day was marked by an annual celebration that is still celebrated by the descendants of the slaves of Upson County. On May 29, 1865, Mr. Cobb declared that the slaves were free in Upson County and the next year on that date the first organized Emancipation Celebration was held.

The earliest newspaper accounted that the first celebration was held near the Central Railroad Depot in area known as White Grove. White Grove was land bought by B. B. White from Isaac Weatherly and Joseph A. (Doc) Weatherly, sla ve traders, and renamed White's Tanner (Happy Hill). White Grove extended from the city water department up Davis Street to the stop sign at The Five Point intersection where Railroad Street (North Hightower Street) and Bethel Street connects. At the old Central Railroad Depot, Victor Thurston credits William Guilford with organizing the first Emancipation Celebration. William was the son of Guilford Speer, born a slave about 1835 in Guilford, North Carolina. The Emancipation Celebration remains the oldest continuously-held memorial of its kind in the nation.

William Guilford wrote there were five speakers: Thomas S. Sharman, Peter W. Alexander, Jennings Thompson, James W. Greene, and (future Georgia governor) James M. Smith. According to the memorial, "the theme of their speeches was advising us to be a peaceable and honest people, and to cultivate a respectful disposition toward one another, and also toward white people." Other eyewitness evidence includes a letter written from Thomaston's James W. Greene on May 30, 1866, in which he said," The freed people had a brilliant Celebration on yesterday."

One early detail of the Emancipation celebrations is absent today. Apparently, Thomaston used to have a cannon-prepared at the militia parade ground, perhaps on the Square. *The Thomaston Herald (June 3, 1876)* reported that "a little after sunrise, the colored people fired one solitary salute in celebration of the anniversary. The shock was sudden and but few understood at once its purpose. Soon the 29th of May was remembered as the celebration of their freedom and the shock was understood if not appreciated." This is the only reference to the cannon.

Some elements of the Emancipation Celebration that have remained unchanged through the years are the official programs of singing and speeches, the reading of the Emancipation, and the happy party atmosphere that attracts thousands of people from miles around.

The Annual Emancipation Celebration was held on Saturday, May 28, 1921, for the first time celebration when the 29th fell on Sunday. It was estimated that from 3,000 to 5,000 Negroes were present. The city was turned over to the Negroes on this occasion and they had full freedom of the streets. Good behavior characterized the events in the past, and it was believed the Negroes would be especially well behaved that year.

The program was prepared as followed: A Song; Prayer by Rev. S.D. Dickerson; "I'll Be Satisfied" was song by the congregation; the President and others made remarks; Miss Carrie B. Sherman read the Emancipation; the guest Emancipation Oration was given by Prof. B.R. Holmes, B.D., President and Founder of Holmes Institution, Atlanta, Ga.; remarks were given by Rev. W.R. Mack, State Lecturer of the K. and P. Jurisdiction of Georgia, and Rev. J.A. Hadley. The General Financial Committee members were Grant Drake, J.C. Banks, A.T. Worthy, (my great-grandfather) H.C. McGill (1921), James Jackson, James Drake, J.W. Stroud, and (my great grandmother) Mrs. Zenobia McGill (1922). G.W. Drake was the president, H. Drake was vice-president; J.W. Stroud was secretary; Rev, S.D. Dickerson was the chaplain; and L.B. Sherman was treasurer of the 1921 Emancipation Celebration.

A search for someone who could remember what the early celebrations were like was found in *Thomaston Times in 1977*, 84 years old Fannie Brown, of 200 Gilbert Street in Lincoln Park. Ms. Brown was the granddaughter of slaves and these were her recollections: "The first time I ever went to the celebration my mother took me by the hand and we walked. We were living on a farm nearby where my father farmed as a sharecropper. I was about seven or eight years old. They were building what we call the Old Mill then and all that section was in the woods.

The speaker's podium was erected in the woods near the Peerless Mill, and tables were placed near the mill for dinner. The guest speaker would tell the people about the *Emancipation Proclamation*, and the old mothers would just shout. Girls from different schools wrote and read essays. People would come in two-horse wagons or buggies, and the train from Barnesville was just loaded with people. Some people who lived a distance would come and spend the night until the next morning. People would bring dinner, and spread it in the woods; some built fires and fried fish. They were crazy about mullet fish.

Some of people never got to the speaking, but would only get as far as town, where the merchants had lemonade stands on every corner. When the people got tired, they would sit on the courthouse lawn on the square, and never hear the real meaning of freedom. The soldiers would come marching from Columbus and the people would follow the band. We did not have floats at first. Back then, there were many buggies and wagons and it was a sight to see.

Her niece, Ida Woodard, who was 74, added, "1923 is the first celebration I can remember. The place where they spread dinner was called 'Old London.' It was in the woods near where the Bleachery is now. I didn't get a chance to get around –I was too little." The Emancipation Celebration event in the community apparently grows more popular as time passes." After many years of Thomaston's first organized Emancipation Celebration, its popularity shows no sign of diminishing.

If you had been a stranger on a bus passing through Thomaston on May 29th back in the 1920s, a startling sight would have met your eyes. The streets of Thomaston were as busy as the streets of New York, and all the inhabitants appeared to be black. Almost every store seemed to have a refreshment stand on the sidewalk in front with merchant's busy serving ice cream and lemonade. It was a hay day of the Emancipation Celebration in Upson County.

Old-timers have said for years that people came from all over the state to celebrate the Twenty-Ninth, and that at one time excursion trains came from Atlanta. Why did the people come to Thomaston? The only answer to that question that was on May 29, 1866, William Guilford organized the nation's oldest continuously-observed Emancipation Celebration, held annually only in Thomaston, Georgia by the black people of Upson County. Therefore, those who had already celebrated at home came to help Thomaston celebrate the Twenty-Ninth in Thomaston. Year after year, they kept coming."

Several thousand Negroes from all section of Georgia and possibly a few from adjoining States celebrated the Twenty-Ninth in Thomaston. The Central of Georgia Railway ran four special coaches for colored people for this occasion, three from Macon and one from Atlanta. A number of speeches by prominent Negroes, several parades, and band concerts were featured in the festivities.

A young woman from New Orleans, Louisianan visited the Emancipation Celebration in 1964, and she was so impressed that she wrote these words to the Thomaston Times: "In the city of New Orleans, world-famous for its beautiful churches and what is the center of an area abounding in natural resources, there live among others, many natives of French descent. As of some others, such as the Chinese and Japanese people now living in the United States, these particular people of New Orleans observe certain customs and traditions of the people from whom they descended. The day of Mardi Gras is one of their celebrated days. It is the last of the several days of fun and festival, which are celebrated in Catholic communities on Shrove Tuesday, the day before Ash Wednesday that is the beginning of Lent. Paris and several other European cities have long been famous for their celebration of it. In America, however, the festival of the "Mardi Gras" is best known in New Orleans. Masks, costumes, parades, elaborate floats, flags, and notice makers are everywhere. In addition, the Municipal Auditorium is the scene of two great fancy dress balls on the night of Shrove Tuesday. Year after year on the very same day, these activities are carried on.

American Negroes also have a day of celebration, Emancipation Proclamation Day. This is the day when all Negro slaves in America were proclaimed free. Abraham Lincoln, then President of the United States, issued this proclamation on January 1, 1863. Negroes in all the counties, with the exception of one or two, in the State of Georgia celebrate on this day. The Negroes of Upson County, the county being an exception, observe May 29th instead of January 1st because it was not until this date that news of the proclamation was received.

There has been much discussion among many Negro s, especially educators and college students, concerning the changing of this day on which the proclamation was issued. Many call the observance of May 29th "out of date", "old fashioned" etc. The writer, before coming to Thomaston had never heard of any county observing any date other than January 1st as Emancipation Proclamation Day. The writer also wished that the Negroes of Upson County would change their date for celebrating the events. However on last Friday, noon, May 29, 1964, as I stood on the corner of North Bethel and Daniel Streets watching the parade, I heard the hearty laughter of the people. I heard their cheers; I saw their action as they erected little tents and made ready their stands for their sales. I saw jolly children running alongside the marching band that led in the parade. However, most of all I felt the spirit of the people. It was a feeling, which I shall long remember. For them, this was not just an annual occasion or mere tradition, this was their deep-rooted heritage, a day on which their own fore parents were freed, not one on which mine or somebody else's were.

Yes, the Negro in Upson could celebrate on January 1st, but I believe that the reflection of their action would only come from the surface and not from deep within. Even the weather is in favor of May 29th; on January 1st the majors and majorettes would be kicking snow. I challenge more young people to take part in the parade to help display the modern day Negro as he holds high positions as city councilmen, county commissioners, judges, congressmen, etc. They must also show how in this great country of ours, "America the Beautiful", that men whose parents lived in the bondage of slavery can hold high positions whose fore parents were kings and queens. Instead of letting the spirit of May 29th die, why not build it up and make the occasion on that day a grand and glorious one. "Let the Twenty-Ninth observance of Emancipation Day be Upson County Mardi Gras".

William Guilford was the owner of 12 acres of land in the city of Thomaston near the Central Railroad Depot, where celebration of the memorial of the slaves' freedom was held on May 29, 1866.

On October 5, 1905 William Guilford, Bob Drake, and Miles Speer were accused of wrongfully and fraudulently taking paper money worth $150.00 from the person of Anderson Pearson-privately, without his knowledge and with the intent to steal. The witnesses against them were Anderson Pearson, Jack Johnson, Emma White, Mark Drake, George Matthews, and Andrew Speer.

Also on October 5, 1905 William Guilford was accused and tried for selling a quantity of alcoholic and intoxication liquor. The witnesses against William Guilford were Anderson Pearson, and Jack Johnson. The defendant, William Guilford, waived his rights to exist in the United States.

William Guilford was indicted by the State of Georgia for selling intoxicated liquor. Guilford pled guilty and was sentenced to work in the chain- gang at the Public Works for the term of six months. The Thirteenth Amendment to the United States Constitution abolished slavery and involuntary servitude, except as punishment for a crime. These 12 acres of land were taken away from William Guilford because of the felony law. William Guilford died in 1908; Thomaston's Emancipation Celebration remains the oldest continuously-held memorial of its kind in the nation.

Georgia, Upson County.

THE STATE
VS
Wm Guilford

INDICTMENT FOR
Selling Intoxicating Liquor
IN THE SUPERIOR COURT OF SAID COUNTY.

Plea OF GUILTY.
Wm Guilford

Whereupon it is Ordered, That the said............................

be and is hereby sentenced to work in the chain-gang on the Public Works for the term

of.........*Six*.........months from the date of.........*his*.........

reception in said chain-gang, and not to be worked anywhere else than on the Public

Works.

The Defendant may be discharged at any time before the end of.........*his*.........

sentence, on payment of the sum of.........*Sixty*.........Dollars

fine, to the proper officers.

This the.........*9th*.........day of.........*May*.........190 *7*

E. J. Reagan

Judge Superior Court, Flint Circuit.

17

Rise of the Cotton Prices in 1900

After the turn of the twentieth century, cotton prices rose and during most of the next two decades they remained high. In response to the improved prices, farmers devoted more and more land to cotton, going from 3.5 million acres in 1900 to a peak of over 5 million acres in 1916. Between 1900 and 1916, the value of Georgia's cotton crop tripling. When American entered World War I in 1917, Georgia farmers experienced greater propriety than any time since the 1850s.

Many things worked against diversification. Force of habit kept some farmers growing cotton because that was the only money crop they had ever planted. Many had neither the education nor financial resource necessary to change from cotton to other crops. Truck farmers, fruit growers, and dairymen had only a small urban population nearby to consume perishable products. Although railroads expanded greatly in Georgia, most farmers did not have easy access to shipping facilities for perishables goods. As late as 1930 only 6 percent of the state's farmers lived near hard surfaced- roads. Logtown Community in Upson County was a prosperous trading center near Waymanville Mill on Tolbert Creek but had no hard surfaced-roads. _The Thomaston Times edition in November 1923 reported,_ Thomaston would soon have another half million dollar manufacturing plant. Plans and specification were being drawn and just as soon as they are completed the actual work of construction would begin. The Bleachery finishing plant and sheet factory would be built by a new corporation which was being formed. The building of the new enterprise would be located between the road leading from the Thomaston Cotton Mills and Peerless Cotton Mills on the south side of the Central of Georgia Railroad from Peerless to Thomaston Cotton Mills. The Bleachery finishing plant and sheet factory would cover a space approximately 100 feet in size and would be two stories in height. The plant and machinery would represent an investment of approximately one-half million dollars. In addition, it will be necessary to erect 50 or more cottages for operatives required in the mills. This means that there would be no lack of employment for carpenters, brick masons and common laborers, both white and black, in the community during the next few months. It was estimated that nearly a year would be required to construct the building and install machinery.

The Thomaston Bleachery was built in 1924 to supply facilities for bleaching and finishing Thomaston products, as well as additional capacity for sheet and pillow case production, commission bleaching, dyeing and finishing.

With the growth of the company, additional housing was needed for workers. Beginning with the construction of the first Thomaston Mill in 1899 to 1918, there was consistent growth. The village that developed around the original Thomaston Cotton Mill was called East Thomaston, and was charted as a separate municipality with its own mayor and city council.

In 1924 Thomaston Mills needed expansion to use the old usual celebration place around the old Central Depot. The Central Railroad Depot was torn down and this area was used to house the Thomaston Mill Bleachery.

Mr. Hillary Cunningham
(1861-1936)

Four years before the Wilson's raid in 1865, Mr. Hillary Cunningham, most professionally known as Mr. Hill, was born into slavery November 10, 1861. Mr. Hill was named after his father, who was also named after his slave-master, Mr. Phillip Cunningham who moved from Buckingham County, Virginia.

The 1870 United State Federal Census showed Hillary Cunningham at the age of ten years old living with his father, Good Cunningham, mother, Susan Cunningham, and his four siblings, Perry Cunningham, Susan Cunningham, Ella Cunningham and Tom Cunningham. Mr. Hill grew in wisdom and statue with all men and fell in love to married Creasy Lue Trippe.

Mr. Hill Cunningham was a very hard worker. His family always taught him to trust in God and to do whatever he had to do to help his people and himself get ahead in the world. This is exactly what he did. Mr. Hill was ambitious with great hope for his own race and tried to uplift his people in every possible way.

Hill Cunningham grew up in the farming community, he owned two grocery stores, and he also grew cotton. Mr. Hill owned a big farm in addition to his own cotton gin on Waymanville Road where he hired other men to work the farm.

In matter of churches and schools he was liberal and never refused when called upon by white or colored people for donations to just causes. Mr. Hill offered to donate as much as $5,000 toward building a church school in the Logtown Community if the Upson County Board of Education matched his pledge.

Mr. Hill's influence was a force, which always uplifted his race. Mr. Hillary Cunningham was an inspiration to the member of both races.

In the 1900s, at 39 years of age, every year when Mr. Hill sold his cotton, he bought a couple of acres of land. In the 1900's, he owned exactly 532 acres of land. In those years everyone had to pay a poll tax, and a lot of people weren't able to pay it because it was very expensive. Mr. Hill was able to pay the price of the poll tax and his land was worth $2,320.00

Thomaston Times, February 7, 1902, reported that Hillary Cunningham brought 286.1 acres of 916.3 acres (or 31%) of Waymanville Mill Property for Two Hundred and fifty dollars and became a stock holder. The sale of the Waymanville Mill Property was the largest public sale ever occurring in this country in the 1900s. In 1911 the mill, land, and machinery were sold to W. L. Duke and moved to Forsyth, Georgia.

Although in 1914, he owned the same amount of land which he did in 1910, the value went up to $19,825.00. The value of the land increased a lot during a very short period of time.

Mr. Hill donated the land and material to build a school across the street from what now is Logtown Bethel Ministry.

H. C. Cunningham Shopping Center in 1936

On the 18th day of September of 1933 Mrs. Creasy Cunningham, the wife of Mr. Hill Cunningham, for two thousand five hundred dollar, purchased from Mrs. Obie McKenzie Black a tract of land in the northern part of the City of Thomaston, Upson County, Georgia. The land commencing at the northeast angle of the intersection Bethel and Daniel Street, and running thence north along the east side of Bethel Street ant to the North side of Daniel Street.

The jewel of Colored Town was the Hill Cunningham Building that was on the west side of North Bethel and Daniel Streets. The Hill Cunningham Building was built in 1933 as an active and attractive shopping strip on Bethel Street, full of businesses owned and operated by Negroes. The Hill Cunningham Building was divided into four sections.

The first section housed the poolroom. A deacon at Macedonia Baptist Church, Mr. Elijah Worthy owned the best entertainment place in town. Worthy's Poolroom was the only poolroom for adult Negro men in town. No children were allowed in this section day or night. Mr. Worthy owned a Negro ballpark on Triune Mill and Pleasant Grove Road where the Thomaston Grays took on other teams of the Negro Baseball League. Mr. Worthy was quite an entrepreneur who owned and drove a school bus.

In the next section, Mrs. Lenny Mae Fletcher owned and operated a café that specialized in home cooked pig ears and chitterlings. We could smell the pungent odor of chitterlings cooking up and down the street all day long. However, at night, when the dancing and the beer drinking started, those chitterlings tasted very good. At night, this area was called "The Block. Everybody wanted to be on "The Block" because that was where they partied. "The Block" was a dangerous place to hang out at night.

The third section of the Cunningham-Hill Building housed a dry cleaner and laundry owned by Mr. John and Mary Reeves, founded by Mr. O.B. Johnson. Mr. James Fagan ran a very popular Snack Bar and Barber Shop for children in the building's fourth section. Day or night children from the neighborhood would cluster in or around the store. Mr. Grover Diggs cut hair along with Mr. Fagan in the rear of the Snack Bar.

Elijah "Lize" Green, Thomaston's oldest Negro merchant and most successful businessmen in the community, was another great and outstanding man who contributed to the development of Upson County. Mr. Green was born in January 1882 to Mr. and Mrs. Isaac Green, a pioneer citizen. Mr. Green grew into manhood in the Happy Hill Community. Mr. Green worked as a porter in some of the downtown department stores. Mr. Green quit Pruitt Murray Company and opened up a business of his own in the Old Number 95 P.B. and S.L. Lodge. In 1908, Mr. Green built and moved into the location on North Bethel Street that is still standing today. The span of more than a half century made Mr. Green dean of all Upson County's merchants and without doubt the oldest business establishment in town. During these years Mr. Green was able to invest; his earning wisely and as a result acquired much valuable real estate holdings in Thomaston.

Mr. Green was a lifelong member of St. Mary AME Church and for years liberally supported church programs. Mr. Green also made large contributions to other charitable institutions. Mr. Green served as co-chairman on a drive which saw more than $7, 000.00 raised for the Upson County Hospital. For sixty fabulous years, the merchant prince carried on a successful business on the corner of Park and Bethel Street. E. L. Green's Grocery Store proudly stood at the intersection of Park and Bethel Streets on the west side.

Mr. Elijah Green was one of the wealthier Negroes in Thomaston. Everybody loved him and his store was a popular spot being located just down the street from the Park Street Playground. After a hard day of playing, children could easily walk there for snacks. Family members worked in the store including Mr. Elijah Green, Mrs. Ida Green, Mr. Joe Worthy, Mr. Edward Worthy, and Miss Lonnie Mae Willis

Mr. Green was laid to rest in the Lincoln Memorial Cemetery, a project which he placed a major role in developing and served as chairman of the board of trustee from the time it was conceived until his death.

Mr. Marvin "Jerry" McGill, my grandfather, and Mr. Alton "Chick" Harris owned and operated this community barbershop. Clarence McGill, my mother's twin brother, cleaned and shined shoes in my grandfather barbershop. Mr. Buster Harp ran the Convenience Store, along with his son, Mr. Milwood Denson and his wife. Mrs. Martha

Ann. Mr. Harp was a deacon and Sunday school teacher at Greater Mt. Zion Baptist Church.

There was, however, an active and attractive shopping strip on Bethel Street, full of businesses owned and operated by Negroes. A beer store was located in the area known as nipperlingsip in the 40's and 50's located in the triangle of Bethel Street, Hightower Street, and Cedar Row.

Just south of the nipperlingsip on the east side of North Bethel Street was Mrs. Rosa Pearson's "Pearson Snack Bar." Her two daughters worked in the Snack Bar and both went on to college and became schoolteachers in Thomaston. The oldest daughter, Mrs. Gussie Flack, taught math at Drake Elementary, and Miss Rosa Pearson taught at Lincoln Park Elementary.

Bentley and Son's Funeral Home was located near Gilford Alley on the west side of Bethel Street. The funeral home, operated by Mr. J. E. Bentley, was part of a chain of colored funeral homes founded by Bentley's father in Reynolds, Georgia. Mr. J.E. Bentley, Jr. migrated to Thomaston in 1955 and opened his establishment first on Drake Street, and later moved to Bethel Street. Mr. Bentley was one of the town's great civil rights leaders.

On the east side of the intersection of Bethel Street stood a café known for excellent hamburger and chicken sandwiches that was owned by Mrs. Doll Murray. Next door to Murray's Café was Mr. Clarence Hanford's shoeshine stand. In the same building was another Negro funeral home owned and operated by Mr. George Wiley Green. A deacon at Macedonia Baptist Church, Mr. Green was a highly esteemed member of the Negro community. For a long time, this was the only Negro funeral home in this area.

A community filling station was located on the west side of Bethel and Daniel Streets. Mr. Benny Jordan and Mr. Charles William were its owner-operators. Behind the filling station was a popular café where you could find the best chicken and pork chop sandwiches, and hamburgers in town. Mrs. Georgia Mae Pearson was the proud owner. My mother, Mrs. Carolyn McGill, was one of the cooks for Mrs. Georgia Mae.

Mr. Milt Wellmaker had a family-run café on Daniel Street near Hightower Street and a third Negro barbershop operated by Mr. Edward "Pig" Barnes and Mr. Albert Grant could be found on the north side of Daniel Street near Hightower Street.

On the east side of Hightower, Mr. Charlie Price, a white man, owned and operated a grocery and furniture store. He employed two Negroes, Mr. Jessie Character and Charles Walker at the store.

The Nina Crawford Café and Harlem Theater were located on the south side of Daniel and Hightower Streets. Mr. Alton Odom, a white man, owned the only movie house open to Negroes in town. The manager was a Negro, Mr. Calvin Murray. The Harlem Theater opened in 1949 with "Gone with The Wind". My favorite movie was "Imitation of Life".

Mr. Andrew S. Johnson opened the Colored Motel on Hosley Street. It had eight units in the motel with hot and cold water, and showers. Each room was outfitted with box spring beds, chairs, footstools, dressers, rugs, and linoleum-covered bath floors. Electric fans and a lamp were provided for each room. There were parking spaces for automobiles. The Motel was located two blocks off Highway 19, one block north of Drake High and Elementary School.

In addition to his agricultural contribution as a farmer, Mr. Hill was affiliated with social events. On the 3rd day of June of 1933, Mr. Hill purchase a tract of land on Triune Mills Road from Mrs. Rufus G. Trice for the sum of Three Hundred Dollar and built a Negro ballpark. The Thomaston Grays of the Negro Baseball League played baseball games in this park.

The Thomaston Grays played in the Branch Rickey Semi-pro League and produced a great numbers of Negroes All-stars from Upson County. Thomaston Grays' managers and founders were James C. Banks, Sr., Albert Walker, and Elijah Worthy.

Thomaston Grays All-star pitchers were Jabb Harris, Houdini White, Milwood Lowe, and Robert Jones. The All-star catcher was Gus Johnson; the all-star first basemen were L. C. Greenwood, Stocky Dixon, and Charlie Howard; second basemen were Clarence McKinney, and Bennie Barnes; the all-star short stops was Milwood Denson ; the all-star third basemen were George Atwater, James Barnes, Johnny Lee Walker, Dick Marshall, and Frank Wiggins; the all-star left fielders were George E. Daniel, and Willie George Hughley; the all-star center fielders Lucian Drake and Earnest Barnes; and the all-star right fielders was Willie Spark.

Mr. Hill along with Henry King, Martin Brown Frank Matthews, and Andrew Fleming organized and sponsored what was known as the

Upson County Fair. The Upson County Fair was located east of town on Highway 74 across from the Upson County Prison Camp. The Upson County Fair was an enterprise owned and managed by Negroes for many years.

The Thomaston Times in July 1936 reported in the death of Hill Cunningham, "colored' Upson County lost one of its most innovative citizen. His life was one that was used as an example for member of both races, white and colored. Mr. Hill was born and reared in Upson County and had lived here all his life which was an open book to the people of the county. Mr. Hill lived honorable upright life and accumulated more than any of his race and more than the majority of the white race. Mr. Hill had the esteem and respect of his own people and of the white race also. Mr. Hill knew his place and was ever respectful to white people who knew and trusted him. Mr. Hill was honorable and upright in all his dealings and accumulated his fortune by industriousness and righteous living.

It was unusual for a member of the Negro race to retain the respect and esteem of both races as did Mr. Hill. Back in the old Jim Crow days before automobiles and other means of rapid transportation Mr. Hill maintained at his home on the farm in Logtown in a lower part the county a room equipped with special furniture, bed linens, and special tableware so that white people who by chance were caught in the vicinity at night could find a place of lodging. Many white people took advantage of his thoughtfulness and were high in their praise of his hospitality. No touch of equality however ever entered into his relationship with white people.

306

STATE OF GEORGIA, UPSON COUNTY

This Indenture, Made the 15 .... day of May .... in the year of our Lord One Thousand Nine Hundred and Thirty Five .... , between Monroe Green, George Gree.., Ulus Green, Len Daniel, ... Earnest Holloway and John Starling, TRUSTEES OF LINCOLN PARK ....

of the County of Upson .... of the one part, and ....
The Upson County Board of Education ....

of the County of Upson .... of the other part. ....
WITNESSETH: That the said Trustees of Lincoln Park ....

for and in the consideration of the sum of Five Dollars and other consideration ....
in hand paid, at or before the sealing and delivery of these presents, the receipt whereof is hereby acknowledged, ha ve granted, bargained, sold, aliened, conveyed, and confirmed, and by these presents, do grant, bargain, sell, alien, convey, and confirm unto the said
The Upson County Board of Education ....

heirs and assigns, a of a certain tract of land lying within Lincoln Park Subdivision, better described as follows, Beginning at the branch on Forest Street which is on the extreme south side of Lincoln Park and extending northward along said branch to Highway which is on the extreme Northern part of the Park and extending along the south side of said Highway to Willis Circle, and then along Willis Circle until it runs into Hill Street, then south to the branch which is on the Forest Avenue, then about twenty feet along Forest Avenue to the starting point, containing around three acres. This land is to be used for school purposes for the children of Lincoln Park and vicinity.

TO HAVE AND TO HOLD the said bargained premises, with all and singular the rights, members, and appurtenances thereto appertaining, to the only proper use, benefit, and behoof of it, the said The Upson County Board of Education, Its successors and assigns, in fee simple; and the said Trustees of Lincoln Park, the said bargained premises unto the said The Upson County Board of Education, Its successors and assigns, against the said Trustees of Lincoln Park, their successors and assigns, and against all and every other person or persons, shall and will warrant and forever defend by virtue of these presents.

IN WITNESS WHEREOF, The said Trustees of Lincoln Park ha ve hereunto set their hand , affixed their seal , and delivered these presents, the day and year first above written.
Signed, sealed, and delivered in presence of.

John Walker

Jno. A. Thurston, N.P.

Upson Co., Ga.

TRUSTEES LINCOLN PARK (Seal)
Monroe Greene (Seal)
Ulysses Greene .... (SEAL)
Lin Daniel (Seal)
John-Starling (Seal) .... (SEAL)
George Green (Seal)
Earnest-Holloway (Seal) .... (SEAL)

B.L. Craxley, ... Clerk

28

THE EMANCIPATION CELEBRATION CHANGED LOCATION IN 1927

In 1924, Thomaston Mills needed expansion to use the old usual celebration place around the old Central Depot. The Central Railroad Depot was torn down and this area was used to house the Thomaston Mill Bleachery and the East Thomaston Ball Park.

The Emancipation Celebration of 1927 was moved and celebrated in the rival communities of Lincoln Park and Harps Grove opposite side of town from the Central Railroad the usual place. On the 29th of May 1927 celebration was located in an area conveyed and deeded to J.W. Starling, G.W. Green, Jr., U.S. Green, and M.O. Green in the Office of the Clerk of Upson County. This location was called Lincoln Park. (Recorded on pages 884-485).

In the 1928-1933, Emancipation Celebration Programs were also held in Thomaston at the Martha Weaver's Park area near the Central Depot. Mrs. Martha Bryan Weaver, grandmother of Mayor Hays Arnold, Jr., respectfully supported the Negroes holding the Emancipation Celebration Program in the park.

This tract of land located in the northeast part of the City of Thomaston, Georgia, and bounded as follow: East by Drake Street; south by Park Street; west by property formerly owned by Lizzie G. Drake, the Mary and Martha Society, and Alton Odoms; and north by Stephens Auto Company, Leon Clem, J.D. Hannah Estate, and the Mary and Martha Society. This tract of land was identical as the tract sold to James R. Atwater by Mrs. Mary Bryan Weaver Arnold, the daughter Mrs. Martha Bryan Weaver, on September 6, 1944 (State of Georgia, Upson County page 433 from 1927 to 1933). A second division of the Twenty-Ninth was held at Martha Weaver's Park. *The Thomaston Time in May 1933* stated there were two headquarters division for the celebration. There was a parade that started at Mrs. Martha Weaver's Park headed by J.C. Banks, and the other parade was in Lincoln Park headed by Rev. J.T. Woodard.

The celebration in Martha Weaver' Park parade in 1929 stared at 10:30 AM. Stared with music by 4th Reg. Band of Macon Ga. The program had a congregational song. Prayer was given by Rev. W.W. Goolsby and selection by the Starr Glee Club. President H.R. Roger delivered a keynote address and then a musical rendition by Starr School and the Macon Band while collection was taken. Miss Willie Dickerson read the Emancipation Proclamation. Eloise McKinney recited the story: "When Uncle Lit Beat that Drum". The Story was followed by lamentations from Dr. H. B. Jefferson, M. D. with Rev. J. W. Guinn, Miss Sally L. Grant, Miss Annie Traylor, Mrs. Odessa Sherman, James Banks, Miss Carrie B. Sherman, Miss Fannie Jones, Ellen Harris, and Florence Mann's.

The Thomaston Time May 1958 stated that weeks of planning by Negroes of this community climaxed Friday with the annual Twenty-Ninth observance of Emancipation Day. The annual observance of Emancipation was completed with a parade and speaking. It was said to be on a broader scale in Thomaston than at any other point in the nation. A parade through the main business section at 12 o'clock noon Friday was formed at the Speaking Ground in Lincoln Park and then moved to North Bethel Street.

Arlie Zorn, president of the Emancipation Day celebration, said "some of the floats met on North Bethel and the rest assembled at the Speaking Ground." After assembling the units were moved to North Bethel for the beginning section of the town, and out Green Street for the return to Lincoln Park. The presiding Bishop of The A. M. E. Church in Georgia, Rev. W.R. Wilkes was the principal speaker.

At least two Negro bands-Drake High School Band and Booker High Band of Barnesville-were in the parade and performed at 1:00 p.m. in Lincoln Park. Monroe G. Worthy acted as master of ceremonies at the Lincoln Park Program. The Negroes of the community surprised Arlie Zorn, In June 1958, with a trophy recognition of 22 years of service as chairman of the Emancipation Day program in Thomaston.

GRANTOR Sells	TO	GRANTEE Buys	INSTRUMENT	DATE Month	Day	Year	RECORDED Book	Page
P. J. Smith and J. T. Galliher, of the County of Upson state of Georgia		Trustees of Lincoln Park and their successors.	consideration of the sum of One ($1) in hand paid and other valuable considerations.	May	28	1927	252	685-6 -689
P. J. Smith and J. T. Galliher, of the County of Upson state of Georgia		Trustees of Lincoln Park and their successors	Said deed was executed for the purpose of and to be used for schools, churches, playground, and swimming pool, and when no longer used for such purpose to revert back to grantors herein and their heirs at law.	May	29	1932	62,	415-4 416
Trustees of Lincoln Park and their successors		The Upson County Board of Education	Education	May	15	1935	65	106
P. J. Smith and J. T. Galliher, of the County of Upson state of Georgia		The Upson County Board of Education	Education	June	9	1950	117	126
P. J. Smith and J. T. Galliher, of the County of Upson state of Georgia		The Upson County Board of Education	Education	September	24	1952	129	10
Trustees of Lincoln Park and their successors		The Upson County Board of Education	Education	October	24	1952	130	177
The Upson County Board of Education		Trustees of Lincoln Park Methodist Church	religion	September	1	1964	194	140
Georgia Education Authority		The Upson County Board of Education	School closing	August	27	1969	210	376
The Upson County Board of Education		Friendship Baptist Church	Religion	March	29	1973	194	140
Trustees of Lincoln Park and their successors George W. Green)		(Ralph H. Martin and Eraest) Emancipation Proclamation Committee in charge of said property	Speaking Ground	November	29	1976	62	
Trustees of Lincoln Park and their successors Sanford Prater, Calvin Ferguson, Ed Walker, William Dawson, Edgar Mahone, J. O. Dodo, Garfield Walker, and George O. Ward		Trustees of Lincoln Park and their successors		July	26	1980	276	820
The Upson County Board of Education		Upson County Commissioner	Quitclaim Deed	July	10	1985	308	552
Upson County Commissioner		Lincoln Park Concerned Citizen George Trice, President	Lessor the annual rent of $1.00 per year	November	15	1985		

Deeds of the Trustees of Lincoln Park and their Successor (1927-1985)

31

THE CRIME TO TEACH NEGROES
TO READ AND WRITE

In the 1860s and 1870s, there was no compulsory comprehensive system of public education for Negroes in Georgia and Negro parents had no way of paying for their children to attend a private academy. As early as 1827, there existed in Upson County what was known as a poor school fund to be expended for the county children.

The term poor fund carried with it no reproach, since all white children of school age were eligible, and attended this school, except those of wealthy parents who could afford tutors. The law provided a small tax, practically all of which was derived from poll tax, to be used for this purpose. Thomas Bethel held the office for a number of years, receiving a five per cent commission on all monies appropriated by the state. It was a crime under Georgia law for anyone to teach a Negro (whether free or slave), to read or write at the end of the civil war. Few Negroes were taught before the war except the members of the households of the largest plantations, who wishes to train them for house servants.

Most people felt that to educate the Negro would make him rebellious; and consequently before 1865 he was given little book learning. This resulted in Negroes illiteracy being even more prevalent than among whites. The education of the Negroes became an urgent priority of the A.M.E. Church. The Negroes had two stumbling blocks in the way of starting their own school: finding money to pay a teacher, and finding a place to hold classes. A local white man reported in 1867: "It seems that a good deal of prejudice exists between the two races, consequently it's a very difficult matter to obtain a house without money that they cannot raise."

St Mary AME Church in Thomaston, Georgia.

By the summer of 1870, Reverend William Harris was sent to St. Mary AME Church in Thomaston, Georgia. Rev. Harris, the third pastor in the history of St Mary, was born free in Hartford, Connecticut, in 1845 but was kidnapped in 1858 and sold into slavery in Georgia. He escaped to the North two years later and eventually enlisted in the Union Army.

William Harris met Rev. M. Turner, a Presiding Elder in the AME Church, on the corner of Peachtree and Whitehall Streets in Atlanta in 1866. Rev. Turner's usual method of recruiting prospects for the ministry was to ask, "Can you preach?" If the answer was "No", he would persist by asking "Can you sing and pray?" If he got an affirmative response, Rev. Turner would scrawl a license for the new minister on the spot.

At the Atlanta Georgia District Conference of the AME Church, Rev. Turner licensed as an exhorter, and then presented him a preacher's license at the Wilmington Annual Conference in Wilmington, North Carolina. Rev. Harris received some schooling at, what would later become, Clarke College. Rev. Harris served Atlanta's Western Mission for two years before being presented a deacon's license in 1870 and appointed to St Mary in Thomaston.

It is safe to assume that Rev. Harris taught school at St. Mary AME Church. St. Mary AME Church had a new church building completed that year which provided ample room for scholars. The school operated in St. Mary at least as late as 1876. Upson County did not open a public school in Thomaston for Negro students until August 1883; St. Mary can confidently claim credit for housing the first successful church school organized for the Negroes in Upson County.

Macedonia Baptist Church Bell of Thomaston, Georgia

This great and historic Macedonia Baptist Church was founded on the 7th day of May in 1870. Macedonia Baptist Church and the nearby St. Mary AME Church were both operating day schools and Sunday schools in 1872. These two churches became pioneers in the education of Negroes in Upson County.

The Negro members of the Thomaston Baptist Church [now First Baptist of Thomaston] determined that it was in God's will that they establish their own church. Macedonia Baptist Church charter members came from their mother church in 1870. Thomaston Baptist Church helped them build their first building. Thomaston Baptist Church gave the Macedonia Baptist Church a bell that now sits in front of the church on Hightower Street. The bell is a memorial of 100 years (1870-1970) existence of the Upson County Negro School System.

The bell was loaned to the Barnesville Church for a year and after a while a proposition to sell it to them was made. The bell was given to the Colored Baptist Church in Thomaston. By August 1870 the bell was hanging in the belfry at Macedonia Baptist Church. Thomaston Baptist Church quickly rescinded the resolution which gave the bell to their black brethren. They substituted the following:

Whereas the Bell was used by Barnesville Baptist Church is now in the possession of the Colored Baptist at this place. Be it Resolved that the Bell be only held by said Colored Baptist Church as a Loan, and to be used by them so long as they keep up the organization of the church and to be returned to this Thomaston Baptist Church whenever it shall become disused for the use of the colored Baptist Church. A copy of this resolution went to Macedonia Baptist church.

Thomaston Star (Starr) School

THOMASTON STAR SCHOOL

The Saturday Middle Georgia Times in January 1881 reported, Dr. J. C. Drake, Wm. Caraway, Wm. Johnson and B.J. Jones composed the Town Council, elected for the ensuing year, sworn in office and the annual supper was held at the Webb House. The Town Council made a donation of $100,000 to the Board of Trustees of Thomaston High School to be applied only to the completion of the school building on College and Daniel Street. Only $3,000 was given to the other colored schools.

The board was commended for making this donation as the education was the paramount interest to the black people of Thomaston and it was to progressive efforts of educating blacks that the town owes its present prosperity and advancement. Let the good work go on. Let our people stand by and uphold the Board of Trustees of Thomaston High School and Thomaston would continue to prosper and grow in wealth and influence.

In Upson County Superior Court during the January Term of 1883, Hyatt Brown, Mumford Drake, Ransom White, Thomas Holloway, Henry Wesley, Wesley Cobb, and Robert Head appeared to petition on behalf of Negro citizens of said county. These men petitioned Thomaston for the education of the Negro school known as the Thomaston Star School. J. W.

Herring, the administrator of Daniel Beall's Estate, sold a lot for $140.00 to Trustees of Star Colored School.

The purchase of the land for the first public school initiated the birth and incorporation of the Thomaston Star School. During the May 1895 term of Superior Court, a petition was filed to increase the number of trustees of Star School from seven to seventeen. The ten Negro men elected and added to the Board of Trustee of Star School were William Guilford, Len Sherman, G.P. Rogers, Henry King, Sharack Drake, Alexander Holmes, Joshun Weaver, Authur Spur, Guilford Guilford, and John Dickinson. Star School was located Town District 561 on the corner of Daniel and College Street.

Miss Carrie B. Sherman, the daughter of the late Levi Sherman, taught at Starr Colored School located on the corner of Daniel and College Street. Miss Sherman taught at Thomaston Training School for many years. Miss Sherman passed in Detroit, Mich. Her remains were brought back to Thomaston for final rites and interment.

In 1912, Mrs. Larcerna Swint Maddox was the first Negro woman principal at Star School in the Upson County Negro School System. Mrs. Larcerna Swint Maddox advanced in age; she quietly lived feebly and alone in her modest home in Greenville, Georgia.

Professor George W. Drake Principal of Starr School

In the 30's and 40's the principal of Starr School was Professor George W. Drake. Mr. George Drake, born June 21, 1879, was another great and outstanding man who contributes to the development of Upson County. Professor Drake, born in 1879 (just 13 years after his parents were freed from slavery) became one of Thomaston's premier educators.

Little is known of his early years, but the 12 signers of an 1880 appeal to the Board of Education urging serious attention to the black schools included four Drakes; apparently his family appreciated the importance of education. The Star School (for blacks) was established by 1883; much depended on voluntary contributions as disbursements to schools were based on the percentage of taxes paid by each race, leaving the black schools seriously underfunded.

Professor Drake attended Star School and then Morris Brown University. He taught in the county schools, and then at Star School for 25 years. His importance for local black education was so great that the Thomaston Training School was renamed Drake School. When the schools were desegregated one of the buildings at R.E. Lee was named the Drake Building. Mr. George Drake was appointed the first superintendent of the Upson County Negro School System and principal of Thomaston Training School.

In 1934, the State Department of Vocation granted the Starr Colored School a Home Making Teacher to teach Vocational Economics, sewing, and other subjects. This was greatly appreciated. Starr Colored School hoped to make that department fit into homes in a beneficial way and to do so, Starr Colored School solicited the cooperation of those who were interested in worthwhile training.

Starr Colored School emphasized Vocational and adult education as never before, because the students began to realize that ignorance was a great curse that existed among them, and the majority of girls and boys who had been academically trained without being taught skills, were liabilities rather than assets.

Don't be misunderstood that our academic back ground is unnecessary and not important, because the literary standard grew higher than ever and to meet the requirement Starr Colored School student must have a better knowledge of higher subjects than a few years ago. It is reasonable to suppose that all the girls and boys of Starr Colored School who were completing school annually would not be able to get jobs upon completion, but if they were taught in school to do vocational work to the extent that could compete with the present day competition, they will be able to find work.

Since home training was being woefully neglected. Starr Colored School took the initiative to prepare girls and boys to fit into our community activities. If anyone had any utensil that they could donate, it would be useful to Starr Colored School in the cooking department. Everyone was encouraged to chip in resources for the school.

In October 8, 1934 Principal George W. Drake of Starr Colored School opened on Monday at 8:30 AM, with the program as follows: Devotional by Dr. G. C. Thomas; remarks, by Superintend Mark A. Smith and an address on citizenship by Mayor H. K. Thurston.

Patrons and friends were cordially invited to attend the opening day. Principal George W. Drake made appeal to the community saying "We are trying to establish a library and any book or magazine you can spare that you think would be helpful to the children will be appreciated. An honorary list of the donors and the title of the books will be kept for future reference. Notify me and I will appreciate calling on you."

Principal George W. Drake, the first teacher of vocational agriculture in Upson County, taught agriculture in the Starr Colored School. Principal George Drake carried the agricultural class to the middle Georgia Vocational School at Fort Valley N. &I. School to hold a judging contest in dairy cattle, utility poultry, and farm crop. The Starr School team, Junior Miller, Junior Brooks, George Mitchell Harris, and Willey Jordan won first honor. Using 300 as a perfect score, Starr School students scored 285; Fort Valley scored 269; and Treutlen County Training School scored 263. In addition to winning the individual prizes the boys won a trip to the state judging contest.

Rural NEGRO Church Schools

There were ten Negro Church Schools in Upson County in 1876. The Upson County Newspaper reported on February 7, 1888, that the Board of Education in session, established Welcome Grove, Job Chapel, Rocky Mount, St. Timothy, and Gray's Chapel Church as Colored Church Schools.

Joe Mims, a Negro, gave one acre of land and a house for a Negro church school to be known as Gray's Chapel Church School in March 19, 1889. This was the first time on record of a Negro man giving land or money for the building of a school. The deed was given to the Upson County Board of Education in consideration of the natural interest that Joe Mims felt for his race. This school was located in the 11th district of land lot #220 about four miles southwest of Yatesville. Georgia. The Negroes of Upson County enjoyed good schools for that day, and they attended them remarkably well during the 1890's. The enrollment in 20 schools in 1892 was 1,345 in 1897 it had increased to 1,734. In 1907 there were 22 colored schools in operation, an increase of 12 since 1876.

These twenty Negro church schools were framed buildings of only one room each with the exception of the Lincoln Park School and the New School. Lincoln Park was a framed building with three rooms and the New School was framed into two rooms. For thirty-two years, Mr. Worthy served as principal of Lincoln Park Elementary School, where Mr. Worthy watched the enrollment grow from seventy students to seven hundred and fifty.

All church school buildings had outdoor toilets and none had running water or electricity. None of the schools had auditoriums or gymnasiums. Most of the seating equipment in the Negro schools consisted of old double-seat desks that had been discarded by the white school. The value of all twenty-five Negro schools was $11,000, as compared to $65,475 for all the twenty white schools. Of the twenty-five Negro Schools, only seven schools were reported to be in good and fair condition.

Eighteen Negro schools were described as very poor or too dangerous to stay in. The two teacher schools had only one classroom, resulting in this unsatisfactory condition with both teachers teaching in the same room at the same time. A flood caved in the porch at the Saga Hill School and the Arabel School had rotted out. The Logtown School was in such a dilapidated condition that it had to be held on braces.

Of the Brown Hill School, Superintendent Smith said: "I don't see how the children keep from dying of pneumonia if they have to sit in the building all day. There are holes in the wall; the windows and doors don't fit and the building was not ceiled at all. Mrs. Alvah Weaver, a white property owner, put a new roof on the Rose Hill School because it was almost like being outside during the rain.

Welcome Grove was the worst school building. The door did not close and the room was dirty and dingy. They had a very poor stove and the stove pipes ran out the window. The window pane was knocked out, causing all the smoke to blow back into the room. There were no desks and the children sat on the benches with no blackboards. Welcome Grove was thought to be a waste of money to pay a teacher for teaching and calling the building a school.

The schools which were termed as being in the best condition were generally the buildings which were also used as church buildings. Eight of the Negro school fitted into this category. One of the major disadvantages in using the church building was that they were too difficult to heat.

Springfield School was the size of a barn that could easily seat 300 students, the children hovered around two stoves and the two teachers tried to teach them together. Most of the schools roofs leaked when it rained, were dirty from smoke, had poor stoves, no blackboards, and not enough benches and seats.

Considering the conditions of these schools in 1940, it was not difficult to understand why so many schools burned down in those times. Most of the building were repaired, provided with better roofs and stoves, and repainted. The minutes of the board of Education contains entries stating that the Pleasant Grove School, which burned in early 1941, was rebuilt, and provided a fire proof roof at a cost of only $500.58.

Partitions were placed in several of the one room schools so that teachers would not have to teach in the same room. By using the old lumber from Union Hill School, which was blown down by heavy winds in 1944, the school was rebuilt at a cost of less than $300.00. Salem School, which burned in April 1944, was rebuilt entirely from funds from the Federal Works Agency.

The Lincoln Park School, which was described as the best of the Negro schools in 1941, burned to the ground on November 14, 1946. The Board of Education replaced the building with two barrack building from Fort Benning, which the Army gave to the Board. The patrons of the Lincoln Park School raised $360 used to have running water piped to the school so that the pupils would not have to continue to go into the yard of a neighboring house to get water from a surface well. The Board of Education helped install the equipment with the understanding that the School would pay the water bill to the city each month.

Generally, the condition of the Upson Negro School system was only slightly improved between 1940 and 1950, as compared to the improvements made in the white.

The number of Negro schools remained at twenty until the 1949-1950 school terms, at which seven schools were closed. The best of the new schools absorbed Rose Hill, Welcome Grove, and Pleasant Grove. Logtown School absorbed Brown Hill. Moore's Crossing absorbed Rocky Mount; Anabel absorbed Pleasant Hill School; and Yatesville School absorbed Sage Hill School.

The board of Education abandoned these seven schools for financial reasons. The State paid $900 for each school consolidation, provided the consolidation would save the state the salary of a teacher. The Board anticipated reducing the number of teachers by six so as to obtain approximately $5,460 additional money from the state.

In 1951, Antioch School closed and the pupils were transported to Yatesville. After completion of the new unit at Lincoln Park in 1954-55, Searcy's Chapel and Cedar Grove Schools were closed absorbed by Lincoln Park. Consequently, the number of Negro schools totaled fifteen. The number did not change at the end of the 1955-56 school years, but at the beginning of the school term in September, 1956, there were only four schools in the Upson county Negro school system.

By 1940 there were twenty-five Negro one- room church schools in the Upson County Negro School System.

1940 Upson County Colored Church School Teacher Director By Superintendent John A. Thurston

School	Teachers	Grades	Enrollment (1939)
Pleasant Hill	Lllian Thomas	1-7	30
Sage Hill	Mattie J. Sherman	1-7	35
Midway	Ora Mae Cook	1-7	41
Yatesville	R.A. Hightower	1-7	96
Allie Price			
Fellowship	Elura H. Collins	1-7	100
W.C. Collins			
Logtown	Edna Kendall	1-7	86
Job's Chapel	Marzilla McCoy	1-7	22
Anniebell	Ora Murchison	1-7	38
Union Hill	Doris Lindsey	1-7	50
Evenly Settles			
Liberty Chapel	Fannie Hicks	1-7	46
Searcy Chapel	Lucile Holloway	1-7	70
The New	Bertha Lindsey	1-7	26
Rocky Mount	Eleanor Settles	1-7	50
Springfield	Susie Protho	1-7	90
Elbert Reeves			
Pleasant Grove	Ruth Hightower	1-7	25
Antioch	Bennie Johnson	1-7	46
Gray's Chapel	Lillia G. Davis	1-7	34
Lincoln Park	Rupert Few	1-7	161
Mattie Jackson			
Sarah Walker			
Monroe Worthy			
Welcome	Carrie Glover	1-7	36
Brown Hill	Lula Walker	1-7	31
Salem	Jimmie Lindsey	1-7	63
Lillie Dixon			
Rose Hill	Mattie Durough	1-7	49

THOMASTON TRAINING SCHOOL

The voters of Thomaston had the opportunity on August 3, 1938, to decide whether the city would build a new Negro High School. City officials placed an advertisement in the Thomaston Times announcing an election to decide bonds for the construction of a new Negro High School a plan in cooperation with the federal government. The school building would cost a total of nearly thirty thousand dollars, and the difference between the bond issue and the total cost being supplied through a grant of the government.

In order for the bonds to be issued, more than half of the registered voters had to cast a ballot for the bond issue, and at least two-thirds of those voting must vote in the affirmative. The voters decided in the affirmative on the bond issues, the city authorities planned to make a tax levy and provide for the collection of an annual tax on all taxable property in the amount that would be necessary to retire the bond as it became due.

On May 5, 1939, The Thomaston Times stated that the new Thomaston Training School was built and keys were given to Mayor Hugh K. Thurston. The contractor for the building was Mr. Ben H. Butts, Jr. The Architectural designer was Robert & Company. Principal George W. Drake was appointed principal of the newly named school, Thomaston Training School, in the Upson County Negro School System.

While the question of equal school for all races is being widely discussed and kicked around currently, the Thomaston Training School, under the supervision of the Thomaston Board of Education, appeared to keep pace with the trends in education. The school house was a spacious, well-constructed, modern building with adequate grounds for recreation and athletics. Several smaller wooden type constructions housed the workshops and a school canteen. The new eight room brick structure was completed with another site about a half of mile northwest of the Old Star School in the Happy Hill Community. This new school was known as Thomaston Training School, and it cost $15,000.00.

1940 Thomaston Training Colored School
Teacher Director
By Superintendent John A. Thurston

1. Professor George Drake
2. Louise Drake
3. Jamie Jackson
4. B.M. Cooke
5. Hiran Virginia Green
6. W.C. Reed
7. Addie L. James
8. Mary Lee Drake
9. Carrie B. Sherman
10. Gussie Mae Pearson
11. Morris Andrew Clarke
12. William James
13. Mattie Lee Barrow
14. Edythe Mae Johnson

The first vocational training course for Negro veterans in bricklaying opened December 1949 on the campus of the Thomaston Training School. Bill Chaney was the first Negro instructor in the Negroes Bricklaying Class, at the Thomaston Vocational School; he was another great and outstanding man who contributed to the development of Upson County. Negro veterans had to apply for training at the white campus of the Thomaston Vocational School. Applications for vacancies for white veterans in machine shop, body and fender, radio repair and auto mechanics were taken also.

The new Negro High School was named in honor of Mr. Drake. Mr. Drake was an educator who served as teacher and principal for more than twenty-five years at Starr School and Thomaston Training School. Mr. Drake devoted forty years of his life-teaching students of his race in Upson County. Professor Drake died May 8, 1951 and was buried in Rocky Mount CME Church Cemetery.

In April 1950, five Negro women organized the Women's Service Group Division for the New Upson County Hospital. Women organized to aid colored patients in the Hospital to enhanced the development of Upson County. The Women's Service Group Division for the New Upson County Hospital officers and member were President Arlene Worthy, Vice-President Mattie McLurkin, Secretary Viola Roberts, Treasurer Lydia Mae Worthy, Chairman of Service Shop Committee Ora Mae Reeves, and Chairman of Membership Committee.

In August 1950, a new and young principal, Professor Charles Julian, a graduate of the Georgia State College with post-grad work in the School of social work at Atlanta University, assumed his duties as principal in September. When Professor Charles Julian came to Thomaston in the fall, the school treasury was about as flat as a pancake, but in his six weeks of office, he had raised funds of several hundred dollars.

A tour of the main school building disclosed a neat and efficiently run institution. The classrooms, some crowded, were all well lighted and furnished. Armchair type desks, that were built to provide more comfortability could be moved around in any desired arrangement, were in all classrooms.

The classrooms included workshops and a chemical and science laboratory. One large room was doubly used as a classroom and an auditorium. The room had a reconditioned piano and was used to store athletics. The institution did not have a library, but Principal Julian undertook plans to make one of the large classrooms double as a library and reading room. The establishment of a library would aid the school in obtaining an "A" rating. The faculty members seemed to be keen and progressive with a deep concern for their jobs and in offering a well-rounded, liberal education program for all the students.

The high school department had an enrollment of about 50 students and about 600 students in the elementary department. There were 15 teachers in the school. The school employed three teachers, Mrs. Hiram Reeks, Mrs. Gussie Flacks and Mrs. Carybelle Sherman, who were all graduates of Fort Valley State College and were natives of Upson County.

Mrs. Mary E. McGill

Mrs. Mary E. McGill, who retired after thirty-three years of service as a teacher, served as an English, French and Social Science teacher at Thomaston Training School, Drake High School, Lincoln Park Elementary School and Cunningham Elementary School in the Upson County Negro School System. Mrs. Mary E. McGill served as supervisor of the chorus, glee club, girl's quartet, the Tri-Hi-Y Club, forensics, and the summer alumna clubs for thirteen years. Mrs. McGill taught conversational French in her class daily.

An outstanding program in the Thomaston Training School was the organization of a school patrol to minimize the number of accidents among students on their way to school each morning. The patrol executed its duties in a noteworthy manner. The Thomaston Training School was not perfect. (Few schools were) There were improvements to be made. After transition from eleven grades to twelve grades in 1952, The Thomaston Training School celebrated it first 4 high school students to graduate from the Upson County Negro school system.

The Thomaston Times in September 1956, stated' "The Negroes of Upson County and the city of Thomaston had school facilities equaled by none and built to last many years. Citizens of this community, interested in the school problem as well as segregation, owe it to visit the new Negro schools in this community. About one million dollars has gone into the building of news schools for the colored children of the community and we challenge anyone to say that Negro facilities are not equal and adequate.

At the Thomaston Training School site a new high school building, more modern than any other school in this entire community, stands ready to give the highest public school education available to Negroes. The building is modern in every respect and facilities within the building are adequate for every course of instruction. The Negroes of the rural areas were now consolidated with the children of Colored town at the Thomaston Training Schools. No longer do they go to one-teacher school where facilities had been inadequate. School busses pick up all those living more than normal walking distance from school and transport them right to the door of the new schools at Yatesville for Negroes, Fellowship and Lincoln Park.

Certainly, no one can say that Negro schools were not equal or inadequate in this community. At this point, they are above equal with the white facilities and certainly adequate having been built to take care of future growth. The finest educational facilities were now available for Negroes that they will prize and cherish and continue questing for knowledge in their own separate facilities.

The athletic program was varied, with a maximum of students participating. The 1956 Thomaston Training School Yellow Jacket, with a veteran football team, was expected to be very competitive. Only four of the twenty-three players on the roster were seniors and this team was not expected to miss the championship and would be even stronger next year.

The Yellow Jackets' Head Coach Curtis Moreland said' "we would have more speed than size and will throw more passes this year." The colored girders opened their 1956 football season on a Thursday night in Barnesville. Five of the nine games on the schedule were played at Lee practice field under the lights. All home games would start at 8:00 pm.

The 1956 Thomaston Training School
Yellow Jackets Football Schedule

September	13	@ Barnesville
September	18	@ Columbus
September	28	Carver
October	5	Hunt
October	11	Staley
October	19	@ Dublin
October	26	T.J. Elder
November	2	@ Forsyth
November	9	(x) Perry

(x) Homecoming

Roman Turmon ---- Center Harlem Globetrotters Basketball Team

Roman (Big Doc) Turmon, made good with the Harlem Globetrotters

The Yellow Jackets' Basketball teams, both boys and girls, won their district championships, and a glass case containing a large number of trophies won by athletic teams of the school is located in the main entrance to the building. Thomaston Training School basketball star athlete, Roman (Big Doc) Thurman, starred with the Harlem Globetrotters, a comedy basketball team, and the Allentown (Pa.) Jets in the Eastern Professional Basketball League.

Big Doc, a graduate of Thomaston Training School and graduate of Clark College in Atlanta, was the pride and joy of the late, Dr. and Mrs. Ollie Thurman, and the brother of Mrs. Ceola Thurman- Drake, retired school teacher from Lincoln Park Elementary School, tour with the Harlem Globetrotters in 1958 and appeared at the Brussels World Fair in New York City to score 68 points in one game. Then Big Doc, standing six feet and four inches and weighting 240 pound, played pivot man for the Allentown Jets in the professional league. He was described as a player who scored rebounds, passes, block shots, and sets up impenetrable screens

Big Doc became a New York Businessman grossing nearly a half-million dollar a year. He left a $16,000 a year professional basketball career to enter business in New York's Harlem. The national Ebony Magazine stated, in two years he owned 2 Chicken Delight Franchises and employed 18 people that grossed $35,000 a month.

Eugene P. Walker, Thomaston Training School football star, graduate with a Bachelor of Arts from Clark College in Atlanta, Certificate in Southern History from John Hopkins University, Master of Arts in History from Atlanta University, and a PHD In History from Duke University. Dr. Walker served with great distinction as the Senator for the 43rd Georgia Senatorial District from 1984 to 1992. Dr. Walker was the first person of color to hold the position of Majority Whip where he was instrumental in garnering support and votes for major legislation in such area as education, health, and the economy.

As a member of the Senate, Dr. Walker served as chairman of the Senate Reapportionment Committee. Dr. Walker was an active member of several civil, community, and professional groups including: the Senate Democratic Policy Committee, Statewide JTPA Committee, and The Georgia Endowment in Education for Humanities, Georgia Partnership for Excellence in Education, and the Metropolitan Atlanta Rapid Transit Authority Overview Committee (MARTOC).

Dr. Walker is also member of the Board of Directors for Literary Action, Inc., the Board of Directors for United Cerebral Palsy, the Board of Director of Shop 'n Check, the Board of Trustees of the John Marshall School of Law, the DeKalb County Chapter of 100 Black Men of America, Inc., the NAACP, and the Butler Street YMCA.

In January 1995 Dr. Walker was appointed by Governor Zell Miller and approved by the Board of children and Youth Services to the position and responsibility to provide supervision, detention, and rehabilitation of juvenile delinquents committed to the state's custody.

The Thomaston Times in January1956, stated' Captain Raymond K. Smith of 414 Drake Street, Thomaston, Georgia, was promoted to the rank of Captain while serving at Amarillo Air force Base, Texas, where he was Adjutant of the 3320th Maintenance and Supply Group. Captain Smith entered the service in October 1951 and was commissioned a Second Lieutenant after graduating from Officer Candidate School in December 1952. He served in Korea from January 1954 until January 1955, and awarded the Korean Service Medal, the United Nation Ribbon and the National Defense Medal. Amarillo Air force Base was the home of the Amarillo Technical Training Command, and was assigned the mission of providing individual training to air Force personnel. The base affords training in guided missiles, jet mechanics, administration, supply and related fields.

In 1958 William Stinson was the first Negro of the Upson county Negro School system to be accepted for a four-year hitch by the U.S. Navy Recruitment Station, another great and outstanding man who contributes to the development of Upson County Negro School System. Stinson, who served six years of service in the U.S. Army, was permitted to bypass Navy recruit training and to be transferred to the Navy Receiving Station at Charleston, S.C. to one of the Navy's ships.

FOUR NEW SCHOOLS

In September, 1959, four new schools were named in honor of outstanding Negro educators from Thomaston and Upson County. The Thomaston Training School was named George W. Drake High School in honor of the late George W. Drake. The principal of Thomaston Training School, Mr. Andrew S. Johnson, remained the principal of Drake High School.

The new elementary and junior high school in the eastern Upson County located in Yatesville, Georgia was named Cunningham School, in honor of and in the memory of Hill C. Cunningham. Mr. L. C. Conn, a teacher and coach in the Thomaston Training School was transferred to serve as principal of Cunningham Elementary School.

Another great and outstanding man who contributed to the development of Upson County was Mr. Walter Collins. Mr. Walter Collins gave his life to the teaching profession in the Crest Community and taught school for forty years; thirty- six of which were in Upson County. He served as principal and teacher at Fellowship for thirty-two years. In addition to his contribution as teacher, Collins donated land included in the school tract at Fellowship Church School. New Fellowship Church School for Negroes, in the western section of Upson County, was named in honor of a living Negro, Water C. Collins. Collins, in his late seventies in 1959, received the honor just a few weeks before his death.

According to _Thomaston Times Colored News on February 1964,_ in a memorial service for the late Professor W. C. Collin held at the Collins Elementary School, Robert J. Reeves, the President of the PTA Council, gave remarks on the life of Professor Collins. Excerpts from remarks by Robert J. Reeves' states, "In every generation there are a few men and women who because of some outstanding attributes such as wealth, philanthropic aim, religious or intellectual achievement, have won the respect and love of their fellowmen. It was these men and women who raise the average of humanity's deeds and brighten the world about them. Such a man was our distinguished citizen, the late Walter C. Collins, for whom this school was named and I was sure the county of Upson and the City of Thomaston are proud to claim as their son.

The story of his life was well known by all of us who are familiar with his achievements and we knew how this school and the church across the street were sacred ashes that have benefited through his generosity. Nonetheless, it was pleasant indeed to hear Mr. Collins attributes praised again by Rev. Martin, who just gave such brilliant account of his many achievements. Born as the son of a sharecropper slave, the future offered little hope for him or any other Nero brought into this world under such unfavorable circumstances. Thousands of bright young men had passed this way since the dark and weary years of chattel slavery and they had not been able to escape the shackles of an environment, which held them hewers of wood and drawers of water and other menial positions in a life where fate was never kind.

He led an exemplary life that young blacks would do well to follow. The man Walter C. Collins whose birth was in the cradle of a community made poor by economics and his subsequent rise to a eminence and wealth in the community was resounding proof where there is a willful faith in God, there is a way. God plays no favorite, and that man is not meant to be a slave to his environment.

In conclusion, Rev. Martin added, permit me to remind you, as Lincoln rose to eminence from Kentucky log cabin to become President of the United States; as Gandhi from a low caste man in India to a place of immortality in World History; as Booker T. Washington rose from slavery to a super place in American education; and as George Washington Carver rose from poverty, Walter Collins, whom we honor, has lifted himself by his own boot straps to a place of eminence among people. I take great delight in honoring Walter C. Collins, teacher of youth, business man, philanthropist, and Christian gentleman."

Only Lincoln Park Elementary would be unnamed until the retirement of Mr. Monroe Worthy. The only living honoree, Mr. Monroe G. Worthy, was so pleased he wrote a letter to the editor, **entitled; "A Negro Speaks Mind about re-naming of three schools."**

Mr. Monroe G. Worthy stated that the announcement which made public the decision of the Upson County Board of Education to honor three outstanding citizens of my race by naming in their honor three of our local schools was received with a deep sense of gratitude. I am indeed delighted at this splendid tribute to the ability and achievement of George W. Drake, H.C. Cunningham, and Walter C. Collin for whom these schools were named. I can think of no persons better qualified to receive this distinguished honor than these three model Negro citizens that the board has so wisely singled out.

It is significant to note, that each of the honorees was born and reared in Upson and chose to cast their lot with those of their own hometown people. The sections as I view them were fitting and proper. Drake, Cunningham, and Collins as the citation so ably pointed out exemplify those traits of character that we would like to find in our people. Each was, or is noted for his rugged honesty, self-reliance, as well as a deep sense of spiritual values which made them humble, yet in that humility there was strength of character which pushed them on to success in their chosen field of endeavor.

We, therefore, congratulate the Board of Education and at the same time express our gratitude to it for recognizing not only these men, but also our entire colored population through its section. These words of felicitation are not from me alone; they are concurred in and by an over-whelming majority of Negroes citizens, for they feel that in honoring three outstanding citizens that it lends dignity to all Negroes throughout the county.

These Negro men symbolize all the hopes, dreams, and aspirations of my people throughout our community. They are the type of men we would want our boys and girls to emulate. The announcement of this honor coming as it does, serves to strengthen the already very fine relationship that exists between the races. It points out the fact more than anything I know that here in the south any person regardless to the color of his skin, if he conducts himself like a man, can command the respect of all people in all walks of life.

The Colored people of Upson County are spiritually richer today because of the honor coming to these men. They have earned and appended to a wonderful heritage for which we are thankful. Again, we appreciate the Board of Education, in so significantly honoring, the men who have contributed so much to their race".

1960 Collins Elementary School
Faculty

1. Principal Marion Underwood
2. Martha Bentley
3. Elbert Reeves
4. Ora Mae Reeves
5. Rev. Ralph Martin
6. Irma Y. Edmondson
7. Roberta Walton
8. Myrtle Johnson Walker

1960 Lincoln Park Elementary School
Faculty

1. Principal Monroe G. Worthy
2. James C. Banks, Jr.
3. Anne Carleen Aiken
4. Carrie L. Glover
5. Ceola P. Drake
6. Amanda J. Green
7. Georgia Nell Henry
8. Ruth V. Hightower
9. Lucile Holloway
10. Mary Alice Johnson
11. Rosa L. Pearson
12. Rosa Mae Jennings
13. Mildred Lindsey
14. Cora Smith
15. Henry Dallas Smith
16. Susie Stackhouse
17. Minnie Lee Tyler
18. Bettie Tripp
19. Lottie M. Wyche
20. Allean Evans

1960 Cunningham Elementary School Faculty

1. Principal Lewis S. Conn
2. Evelyn Settles
3. Ora Bell Sullivan
4. Littie Mae Taylor
5. Mary McCoy Traylor
6. Joe E. Worthy
7. Crawford Atwater
8. Gloria Lyles
9. Bessie Walker
10. Carrie Walker

HOUSING AND GOVERMENT

My family lived in Colored Town where my mother, Miss Carolyn McGill, like so many Negro mothers, had to work long hours for little pay in white homes in order to support the families. My mother worked very hard as a domestic employee in order to raise her four children, Diane, Cornelius, Marvin, and Jeffery in the Colored Town neighborhood. We grew up in a small alley called Guilford Alley. This was a dark alley with no lights on the street. There were five shotgun houses near the Church of the Living God Sanctified Church. These houses were called shotgun houses because they had only three rooms and a front porch -- you could shoot a gun through the front door and it could exit a window without touch anything.

The first seventeen years of my life were spent in a typical three-room shotgun house with no indoor plumbing; the only heat was from a fireplace and our lights were kerosene lamps. The bathroom was on the back porch but we had no bathtub or running hot water. To take a bath, we heated water on a wood stove, then poured it into a big tin tub. The windows were single hung from the top. We would raise the bottom sash and put a stick of stove-wood beneath the sash to keep it up. Without window screens or backyard privies, we had an abundance of flies.

James McGill

At our house, six family members lived in three rooms. My mother slept in the front room. There were three beds in the middle room. Uncle John Dawson had a bed; my two brothers and I shared a bed and then Uncle Rufus Atwater slept in a bed. Uncle John would spread newspaper on the floor each night so he could spit out his tobacco juice. That was okay because he was the main breadwinner. He would make sure that we had food to eat, wood to cook with, and all the bills were paid. Uncle John was the heart of our family.

Life in Colored Town was very close and few secrets could be kept. Houses were so close together that when neighbors walked by talking, it seemed like they were inside the house. Even though the community was all Negro and very humble, residents did not own their homes. Once these houses were built, they received very little, if any maintenance. In due time because of lack of funds and effort, our community deteriorated into a slum area.

In November 1961 a group of Negro citizens of the community filed a petition asking for improvements in living and recreational facilities as well as street improvements with the Upson County (White) Ministerial Association. The Upson County (White) Ministerial Association members were Rev. W. H. Ruff, Rev. Edwin L. Cliburn, Rev. David Payne, Rev. Thomas M. Dews, Rev. Wesley L. Thomas, Rev. R.B. Collins, Rev. Robert Kent, Rev. Reno Davis, Rev. Pierce Wilcox, and Rev. W. P. Perry. These ten local white ministers filed an answer with the Negroes to their petition and city officials for the Negroes to come before the mayor and council to work out plans with the Negro leaders.

In the meantime, the Negroes received commendation from white ministers of the community for their sincere concern for the betterment of the colored race. Investigation of the petitioners had revealed that it was purely a local level matter and was free of outside advice or interests. In a letter signed by ten local white ministers the Negroes were commended "for their desire to see their race lifted up."

"To the Colored Citizens of Thomaston and Upson County

"We the undersigned ministers of Thomaston and Upson County are cognizant of your petition to the City Council categorically out lining the conditions and needs physically, morally, and educationally of your race here in Thomaston. It is not our desire to act subjectively on your petition, but simply comment you for your desire to see your race lifted up. You have made progress in recent years- we are proud of your public schools with adequate class rooms in good repair; a and other facilities that denote progress-but this is not enough. "

"We believe you are justified in your requests and sincerely believe that our City Fathers will make every effort to meet these situations and effect long range planning to help you to lift higher the moral, academic, and spiritual conditions of your people. As ministers, our chief interest in the community is moral and spiritual, but we realize that the physical, moral, and education, all must be included to achieve our aims. When your peoples' morals, ethics, health, and education are substandard, the whole community suffers. When you progress, then we are all better. We commend you for your sincere concern for the betterment of the colored race. Even though progress has been made here, and all across our state, let us appeal for earnest prayer, genuine understanding, and diligent work in creating a better community for all of us as well as those who will come after us."

City officials gave an attentive and sympathetic ear to Negro leaders who came before the mayor and council to voice requests they had earlier written for community improvements. Monroe Worthy, Negro school principal and businessman, personally wrote to the council "every word in the petition and the request was purely local with no outside interference or assistance."

Mayor Harvey Green and the council told the Negro leaders a committee had been appointed on Urban Renewal, which would cover most of the requests they had made. In general, the Negroes were told the city would "help all they could" by Mayor Greene.

The city attorney proceeded with plans to amend the city charter whereby citizens of Thomaston may continue to vote directly on the office of mayor and condemnation of 45 Negro houses. The mayor and council instructed the city attorney to prepare an amendment to a 1938 sanitary ordinance to make possible condemnation of all property not meeting minimums sanitary requirements.

An amendment to the present ordinance is necessary to cover property without minimum sanitary toilet facilities, but not within the reach of city sewerage. Owners of forty-five Negro houses without minimum sanitary toilet facilities and two business establishments in the same category got attention.

Mayor John Edenfield told city council to study the public housing and asked the councilmen to join him in further study of a local public housing project. The mayor told councilmen that he already visited in a number of communities with public housing and talked with officials concerned with it. He asked the other city officials to research the reported conditions. Thomaston's Chief Executive also said he would arrange for someone in an official position to come and explore the public housing program and discuss a rehabilitation program.

Public housing was worked out in two ways, through private enterprise, or through a municipality public housing. Apparently, Mayor Edenfield was considering the possibility of a municipal public housing authority, which could borrow one hundred percent financing from an agency of the federal government to build rental property for low-income families. Several communities in this area of Georgia have Public Housing Project, including Talbotton and Griffin.

Thomaston Times reported on June 17, 1971 that Urban Renewal seemed within reach in Thomaston, and Mayor John Edenfield and the city council accepted appraisals of 49 parcels of property to be bought in Drake heights. Thirty-one parcels were not approved but would go to a third appraiser for approval. These 31 were described as varying more than twenty percent between the high and low appraisal of local appraisers. The 49 did not vary more than twenty percent.

Mayor Edenfield said that the parcels were approved and the amount would not be made public immediately. Instead, after acceptance, the Thomaston Urban Renewal Department forwarded the list to HUD in Atlanta for final approval. Money was in hand to buy parcels of property running in the area north of Holsey Street that was in effect. The land would be cleared, streets resigned, and the property put back on the market for planned development. The 31 unopposed parcels of property were being studied by the third out-of- town appraiser, and presumably would be ready for acceptance at an early date.

Thomaston Housing Authority Director Billy Reeves, the first Executive Director and Administrator, devoted some time to assisting

City manager John Baxter in the Urban Renewal Department, and Mrs. Billy Adams was a full-time employer in the office opened at City Hall. It was anticipated that in April 1964, Public Housing for low-income families in Thomaston would soon become a reality.

The Urban Renewal program exceeded $1 million dollars, the majority which was paid by the federal government. The Thomaston Authority became chartered and established in 1967 on a 30-acrec site on the Triune Mill Road, on the tract that was made by the Industrial Authority, which bought the land from James W. Ferguson.

There were some 200 housing units in the development, and 40 went to elderly citizens and 160 went to low-income families. The area west of Five Points, known then as Happy Hill, was cleared under the Urban Renewal program. The families from the Happy Hill Community were transferred to the newly established Triune Village Housing Community in 1969.

The Happy Hill Community name was changed to Drake Height Community, and the Urban Renewal reestablished the tract for elderly citizen's housing and private homes in 1976. The Urban Renewal and the Thomaston Housing Authority established a housing community in Lincoln Park in 1981.

On June 15, 1962, The Citizens Southern National Bank, acting as Trustees under the will of James R. Atwater, sold the land to the City of Thomaston and changed the name from Martha Weaver's Park to Park Street Playground. This land was located at the northwest corner of Park Street and Drake Street, which had been used by John Drake and the Negro Community as a playground since April 19, 1955. (Recorded in State of Georgia, Upson county, page 524, on June 15, 1962).

James C. Banks, Jr.
Math Teacher and Coach at Lincoln Park Elementary

The Thomaston Times in October 1963 reported the City Officials met with the leaders of the Negro Community to propose to locate a pool adjacent to the Drake High School Gym. The officials offered to put $10,000 into the swimming pool and another $10,000 from Thomaston Mills that was pledged if the Negroes raised one-third the cost of their proposed $30,000 swimming pool by November 24 of the following year. The majority of the Negro leaders agreed in the presence of the City Officials, but after the meeting most of the Negro leaders wanted the lemonade, but did not want to squeeze the lemon. Chairman Monroe Worthy blamed a little bit of apathy as reason they did not want to measure up to expectations. He had faith that some were interested and would work. The women and educators of the Negro community began to plan and work hard to raise the funds. James C. Banks and H.D. Smith organized a salvage committee to pick up waste deposits next door to Green's Funeral Home on North Bethel Street... Co-chairwoman Julia C. Martin held a singing and baby contest at Macedonia Baptist Church. Rev. Marion Underwood, principal of Cunningham School, held programs at the school. Ora M. Kendall, teacher at Lincoln Park Elementary School, turned in donated checks. Britt Manufacturing donated $594.00.

The new $30,000 Negro swimming pool was completed and dedicated in October 1964. The pool was located adjacent to the Drake High School and was operated by the school's physical education department during school months. The Drake Swimming Pool Committee consisted of Monroe Worthy, chairman, Julia E. Martin, vice-chairman, Elijah Worthy, Albert Walker, George I. Jennings, H.D. Smith, James C. Bank, Jr., Ollie Thurman, and A.S. Johnson.

One of the biggest stories of the year was the successful completion of the Drake High School Sport Complex. A Sport Complex with a metal and masonry building with a gymnasium with dressing rooms, a basketball court, a football field and a new $30,000 swimming pool located adjacent to the gym dedicated in October 1964. The sport complex was operated by the school's physical education department during the school months

The Negroes history of Upson County accounted for some big stories that had a tremendous bearing on the civic, religious and cultural behavior of our people. The Fathers of the City of Thomaston looked for the Negroes' interest in 1962 by purchasing from the Citizen & Southern

Bank, acting as Trustees under the Will of James R. Atwater, deceased, a tract of land identified as Martha Weaver Park for $9,500. Mrs. Martha Weaver gave John Drake permission to organize and used the land for a Negro Community playground in 1955. This land was located at the northwest corner of Park Street and Drake Street, which has been used by the city of Thomaston, Georgia, under lease from James R. Atwater, as a playground. This tract of land is known today as Park Street Playground.

LOOKING ON the new Recreation Center for Negro Teen-Agers with deep interest are E. L. Greene and Mrs. Elnora Collins who gave $100 each to the project located at the Park Street Playground.

The Thomaston Times edition in February 1963 reported, Mrs. Viola Roberts, Mary A. Johnson, and Ola M. Reeves of Thomaston, attended the Federation Club (name change to Boys and Girls Club of America in 1990) in Macon, Georgia and charted a Women's Federated Club. In February 1963 a house was donated to the Women's Federated Club by the city that was located on Park Street Play dedicated to be a Youth Center for Negro youth. The young people needed a positive place to grow.

The Thomaston Times in March 1962 stated: Upson County could not be exempted from the U. S. Vote Bill because fifty percent or better of Negroes had not been registered since last general election. Thirty Negro students in Social Science classes from Drake High School were registered to vote in county, state and national elections. Seventeen of the groups also qualified to vote in city elections. The history class of Eugene Pierce Walker came to the courthouse in two groups, and Mrs. M.B. Maxwell, the county registrar, said that thirty of thirty students passed the test to register and become qualified voters. The students had studied government and the registration was part of the study. Similar projects had been carried out in previous years. Registration was carried out six days a week on the third floor of the Upson County Courthouse. Citizens walked in to register regardless of color, which was a simple procedure. The questions asked each applicant were:

1. Have you lived in the state one year or in the county for six month?
2. Are you registered to vote anywhere else?
3. Do you want the literacy test- a simple demonstration to prove your ability to read and write?
4. What body can try impeachments of the President of the United States?
5. If a person charged with treason denies his guilt, how many people must testify against him before he can be convicted?
6. At what time of day on January 20 each four years does the term of the president of the United States end?
7. If the president does not wish to sign a bill, how many days is he allowed in which to return it to congress for reconsideration?
8. If a bill is passed by Congress and the President refuses to sign it and does not send it back to congress in session within the specified period of time, is the bill defeated or does it become law?

Those who could not read and write, however, usually took an alternate test. The registrar had preprinted cards containing phrases from the Georgia, or U. S. Constitution, which they gave people to read. The longest had twenty words, the shortest, about ten words,. and the card was picked at random. Provided one could read the simple phrase on the card, Negroes were then asked to write the phrase. Those who were unable to read and write were given an oral test. They were asked twenty questions of which they were required to answer fifteen of them. Some questions were; (1) Who is the president? (2) Name Georgia's two senators, (3)Name the state representative (4) Who was the sheriff of Upson County? The test included other similar questions.

Passing either the literacy test or question-answer test brought the registrars to the point of asking, 'Have you ever been convicted of treason, embezzlement of public funds, bribery or larceny or any crime involving moral turpitude? Anyone who reached this stage was ready to take the oath that they were a citizen of the U. S. state, eighteen or older, and they had met the requirements of the test. After that, they signed a card with passing noted on it by the board of registrars, and they were given the procedure by the registrar to vote.

The year of 1964 saw the paving of most of the streets in Colored town. The filling up some of our mud holes at the same time eliminating a few dust bowls.

In May 1964, *according to the Thomaston Times*, every street in the Negro residential section of Colored Town was paved. Only the streets that were too narrow that road equipment could not move through were omitted paving. The streets were made paved through the cooperation of county officials who made the new, county-owned paving equipment available for the city use.

County Commissioner Hays Arnold said that "they recognized the fact that the County of Upson collected taxes in the City of Thomaston, too, and they were happy that it was possible for the county to assist in this paving to the extent of making county equipment available. Because they were able to work it in to their schedule while roads were being readied for paving, it did not cause any inconvenience and did not hold up any county road paving."

A free verse was written by Mrs. Zepherine Roper to express gratitude to the city fathers for the street improvement which took place in the colored section of town:

We saw you when you were in a rut
On sunny days we despised the looks of you
On rainy days you were muddy we were afraid that should we
travel we would slide into the ditches that lay by your sides.

What an awful condition you were in
It seemed as if you were just going to run down and down
Then one day we saw men digging close beside you,
And all along your side they placed sturdy stone walls.

The City of Thomaston increased police manpower in June 1965 with the addition of the three new Negro Officers, George Trice, Jr., Harold Jackson, and Jack Lockhart. These were the first three Negro policemen in the history of the City of Thomaston. A city official said that the three Negro policemen were trained, provided with their patrol cars, and worked as a team in the Negro section of Thomaston.

The Thomaston Times in October 1967 edition stated, residents responded favorably to a request at the Monroe G. Worthy P.T.A. meeting that porch lights be turned on regularly in the area to make it a safe place. Sheriff E. T. Bray had called for lights in Lincoln Park "to protect the good people in Lincoln Park" who had been victims of muggings as they walked the dark streets. Sheriff Bray, who then had a sheriff's patrol working Lincoln Park on a regular schedule, said that the patrol would be more effective since the dark streets were to be lighted.

Lincoln Park was an unincorporated area. In November 1967 there was high praise of the cooperation from R.E.A in bringing a possible solution that had plagued the citizens of Lincoln Park for some time. The problem had grown increasingly worse in recent months. The 2,000-plus populated area was without a single public light. Street lights that were mercury vapor, bullet-proof, and sufficient to light the entire area of more than 500 houses were turned on.

In October 1968, Thomaston's first Negro council candidate in the history of city elections was Andrew S. Johnson, principal of Drake High and Drake Elementary School since 1951. Mr. Johnson was manager of a district insurance office in Athens prior to entering the education field. Mr. Johnson was married to the former Mary A. Stone, -Johnson's had two children, Veronica and Andrea Johnson.

Mr. Johnson was a Baptist and was also member of the Progressive Men's Civic Club, Non-Politician Voters Council, Alpha Phi Alpha fraternity, a Mason and Shrine. He held a pre-medical B.S. degree, a Principal's Certificate, and M. A. degree in Administration and Supervisor Education.

He also was working on his doctorate at New York College. He had been Negro Chairman for the Polio Drive for ten years. Mr. Johnson promised "service for all of Thomaston and that the city image would change."

In July 1968, J. E. Bentley, Jr. was the first Negro to seek office in the Upson County government since reconstruction days. Mr. Bentley, a businessman and civil leader, ran for the office of justice of the peace in the Town District. Voting on Mr. Bentley's office was not to be count-wide, but would be restricted to Town District where Negro voting ran as high as fifteen and twenty percent. A licensed embalmer and funeral director for nineteen years, the justice of the peace candidate's wife, Martha, had one child, Raymond Bentley. Raymond Bentley was schooled at Fort Valley State College for three years, and graduated from the Atlanta College of Mortuary Science in Atlanta, Georgia. Mr. J.E. Bentley Jr. was in the military, and served and fought in the Korean conflict. Mr. Bentley was a member of the Greater Mt. Zion Missionary Baptist Church, but stressed that he was active in all churches, civic and social groups, and supported them fully." He made it perfectly clear that if he was elected Justice of Peace, he would crack down on any riots, looting and burning. He pledged his support to the cause of justice and peace in Upson County for all people. He sincerely promised justice to all, and maltreatment toward none. He sincerely promised stein treatment to all who participated in looting and burning.

In July 1972, Bill Wright, a native of Monroe County, but a naturalized Upsonian for fourteen years, announced his candidacy for the office of Coroner. He had received his formal education from Hubbard High School in Forsyth, Georgia, Atlanta College of Mortuary Science in Atlanta, Georgia, American Academy of Plastic Surgery in New York, N.Y., and attended Morehouse College for two years. He was the Mortician in charge of Lincoln Memorial Chapel in Lincoln Park.

Mr. Wright worked with Coroners and pathologists for 32 years in approximately 40 counties in the state of Georgia performing autopsies and assisting the respective officers in their designated fields. He was the President of BLBP Organization of Lincoln Park, President of Lincoln Park Social and Saving Club, member of Dumas Lodge F&A.M. of Thomaston, a licensed and ordained Baptist Minister, and a member of Welcome Grove Baptist church in Thomaston.

After graduating from Thomaston Training School and Clark College in Atlanta, Georgia in 1958, Eugene Pierce Walker returned to Thomaston to join the Drake High School staff as a history teacher, and to serve as assistant line football coach on the staff of Coach Earnest Tolbert's Drake High Yellow Jacket Football Team. Coach Walker remembered a historic tract of land sold to James R. Atwater by Mrs. Mary Bryan Weaver Arnold, the daughter Mrs. Martha Bryan Weaver, on September 6, 1944 (State of Georgia, Upson County page 433). The land that was developed by a Negro, John Drake, who returned home from military and was a community active, had been used as a playground since April 19, 1955 that was owned by James R. Atwater. The lot fronts was 400 feet, more or less, on the north side of Park Street and fronts 240 feet, more or less, on the west side of Drake Street.

Coach Walker's first agenda was to organize the Park Street Playground into play-offs to determine colored children champions in badminton, ping-pong; horseshoes, little and junior league baseball were underway at the Park Street Playground for Thomaston and Upson County. In the Thomaston Times, Eugene Pierce Walker, director of the playground, said, "We will have games and activities at the park throughout the summer and I would like to invite everyone to come out and see our play-off.

We would especially like to see the parents of the children taking part in the activities come out and support their youngsters." Badminton, ping-pong, horseshoes, and volleyball were played at the Park Street Playground each day. Girls Softball Baseball games was played by the city each afternoon Monday through Wednesday. The Crusader's Club of the Macedonia Baptist church served refreshments during the play-offs. The first place winners received awards.

On Friday evening a junior league baseball game was played between the Braves and the Cards at the Park Street Playground. The winner of the best of three out of five games played for the champion. The Boy's Club played a baseball game against the Thomaston Sluggers at the East Thomaston Ball Park each Monday evening.

Coach George Edward Daniel led the Thomaston Boys Club Pony League Team to a 15-6 record into the state tournament. Pitcher Edward

White led the Club with an 8-1 record. Then on Sunday afternoon the Little League and Junior baseball teams traveled to Macon to play a pair of baseball games.

Jim Brown, baseball chairman for the Junior League Baseball program of Thomaston, attended the organization meeting Sunday, April 4, 1965 at the Barnesville Youth Center to get formation about the Middle-Georgia Pony and Colt League Baseball Program.

The Thomaston Times edition in April 1965 reported, Jim Brown and James Harris held an organization meeting at the Park Street Youth Center for the formation of the Middle Georgia Pony and Colt League Baseball program. The Officers was elected: President Sammie Johnson of Jackson, Vice-President Jim Brown of Thomaston, and Robert Myles of Barnesville and Treasurer R.M. Matthews of Griffin. The program called for $5.00 for group insurance and a $9.00 certification fee. The board during their two and one half session also discussed the possibility of entering an All-Star in the National Pony League Annual Tournament. However, the details were not released until further information and facts were studied.

Each team played the following games:

May 8th
Thomaston at Jackson
Griffin at Barnesville
May 15th
Barnesville at Thomaston
Jackson at Griffin
May 27th
Thomaston at Griffin
Jackson at Barnesville

In August of 1965, the Little League Baseball Tournament was held at the Park Street Playground Field. There were teams from Griffin, Barnesville, Jackson, Talbotton and Thomaston competing. The Campanella Stars of Griffin and the strong Colts from Barnesville were considered favorites in the tournament.

According to Chairman Jim Brown, "this was the first organized baseball tournament for boys between the ages of 9 and 12 to be presented since the inception of boy's baseball in 1957." Coaches James Harris and Jim Brown's guided the Thomaston Cardinal in the championship game against the Barnesville Colts. They were led by the timely hitting of James McGill and the pitching of Milton "Smokey" Mobley. Pitcher Smokey Mobley pitched a great game against the Barnesville Colt. The All-star catcher James McGill, the offensive star for the Cardinal hit a walk off two run homer in the final inning to give the Cardinal a 6-4 victory over the Barnesville Colt and the championship.

All activities on the colored playground were sponsored by The City of Thomaston Recreation Department. The Mayor and Council of City of Thomaston voted to financial support of the programs. The city officials voted to put $500.00 from the money from parking meter revenue into the Park Street Playground programs.

Principal Andrew S. Johnson

DRAKE HIGH SCHOOL (1958-1970)

The Thomaston Times1958 edition stated that on a Sunday in May there was a big day for the Negroes in the Upson County Community. Principal Andrew S. Johnson, along with Otis Frank Wiggins President of the Drake High School Student Council, and the Student Council Advisor Mrs. Mary E. McGill called their white friends, members of the immediate family of the late George Drake, and the entire community to officially dedicate the new section of the school, and confirm the decision of the Board of Education to rename the school.

Principal Andrew S. Johnson, the first and only principal of the newly named George W. Drake High School, said "there were reserved seats for the white people and several short statements were offered". This statement came from prominent Negro leaders including Ollie Zorn, T. W. Hobbs, Sr., Rev. C. H. Atwater, Mrs. Ora Reeves, Mrs. Edith Johnson, and Mrs. Mary E. McGill. City and State school officials, a member of the Thomaston Board of Education, and the contractor of the new building were all part of the program. L. H. Pitt, Secretary of the Georgia Teachers and Education, was the principal speaker. The Drake High School Band played several selections with President of Student Council Otis Frank Wiggins extending the welcome. The ceremonies started at 3:00 p.m., and open house of the school followed.

The school, formerly Thomaston Training School, was renamed Drake High School in memory of the late George W. Drake. Mr. Drake was a Negro educator that served as a teacher and principal for more than twenty-five years. He devoted forty years of his life teaching bright black faces in Upson County.

In August 1958, construction was expected to begin on a $50,000 gymnasium for Negroes at the Drake High School. The gymnasium would be a jointly financed venture for the City of Thomaston, County of Upson, Thomaston Mills and Martha Mills. Several other school projects have been similarly financed. Financing for the gymnasium was worked out with the four cooperating groups by a Planning Commission appointed some time ago, to study plans and means of financing a gymnasium for the Negroes.

Dickson Adams, chairman of the Thomaston Board of Education, as well as chairman of the Planning Commission said "the gym has been made possible through the fine cooperation of these groups just as many project before." The gymnasium, to be the first such building for Negroes in the community, will be located on the campus of Drake High School. The gym will be constructed as a metal and masonry building.

The gym will have dressing rooms for the boys and girls and a playing floor for basketball. The building will be used for basketball games and for physical education classes. Permanent seating facilities have not been planned now. The building will be sixty feet by one hundred and twenty feet, and the four cooperating groups will share the estimated $50,000 cost equally.

Thomaston Times stated on October of 1958," the first Drake Yellow Jacket Football Team, after changing from Thomaston High School, was ready for the 1958 homecoming football game. High spirits and wild enthusiasm were felt throughout the campus during the Homecoming week. All were anxiously waiting for the 4 o'clock homecoming parade on Friday evening. There were floats, queens, bands, and more queens."

The high stepping majorettes of the Drake High School and Elementary Bands, along with the Knight High School Band from LaGrange preformed. The parade left the campus of Drake High School, traveled up Hightower Street, went up East Main Street to circle the Courthouse, turned onto South Bethel to North Bethel, and returned to the school campus.

The parade led up to the game Friday night, Drake High vs. Houston County Training School from Perry, Georgia, 8 p.m., admission .50 in advance and $1.00 at the gate. During the half-time period, the Primary (1-3 graders), Elementary (4-7), and High School 1 each performed. The fast stepping Drill Team from the Physical Education Department marched. With high spirits, charming queens, and a well-trained team, we were sure to win.

The Drake High Yellow Jackets' Head Football Coach, Earnest Tolbert, assistant and line Coach Eugene Pierce Walker, stated that Frank Wiggins, 175-pound halfback, would serve as captain of the Yellow Jackets. The Drake coach singled out Lonnie Gray, 180 pound halfback and Wilbur Ivey 175 pound quarterback. Probable starters for the Jackets Friday night against Houston County will be Ivey at quarterback. Wiggins and Gray at the halfbacks. Elizah Herndon (175) will be at fullback for the Jackets. Tommy Dawson (160) and J.C. Carson (180) will be Drake flanks. Tackles are Benjamin Rogers (205) and David Walker (170). Walter Rogers (200) and Gene Johnson (170) are likely guard starters. Horace Jackson (170) will play the center spot in Drake line. Other members of Drake football squad are Tommy Martin (175), Maurice Worthy (165), Nelson Acey (165), Junior Carson (175), J.D. Hill (160), Monroe Banks (145), Wilson Smith (145), Calvin King (160), Jesse Chapman (160), Archie Townsend (179), James Drakes (150), Eddie Pickard (175), and Milton Davis (165).

In April 1959 Lincoln Park won the girls' colored basketball tournament, while Collins boys came out on top in the boys at the new Drake High School Gym. The tourney games were the first basketball games played in the new Drake High School gym. In their opening game, the Lincoln Park girls were defeated 35 to 10 and then came back to plaster Cunningham 34 to 27 and walked off with top honors in the girls' division.

The Collins quintet clipped Drake 43 to 26 in their first game and edged past Lincoln Park 47 to 41 to win the boys tournament. Cunning gained the final round in the girl's tourney with a convincing 26 to 15 over Collins. The Lincoln Park boys won second place after a 49 to 39 win over Cunningham only to bow in the finals to the strong Collins boys.

Immediately following the games the trophies were awarded to the various teams by Superintendent Gordon Holston. Drake's Principal, Andrew Johnson, said, "He wanted to thank the Superintendent, Board of Education and, all the citizens of this community for this modern gym."

1960 Drake High School
Faculty

1. Ruby Allen
2. Roumal Bivins
3. Pauline Blasingame
4. Charlie Brown
5. Patricia Carter
6. Savannah Cook
7. Dorothy Denson
8. Gussie Flacks
9. Mattie Ivey
10. Roosevelt Jacks
11. Rufus Jackson
12. Pauline James
13. George Jennings
14. George Jowers
15. Fannie Leary
16. Juanita McMillan
17. Cleopatra Miles
18. Morris Brown Patterson
19. Dora Mae Ross
20. Mattie J. Sherman
21. Alice Smith
22. Johnnie G. Taylor

23. Isaiah Terry
24. Earline Vaughn
25. John W. Vaughn
26. Eugene Walker
27. Janet Wallace
28. Evangeline Williams

In the August Edition in 1961 in the Colored News of the Thomaston Times George W. Drake High School sports reporter, Arthur Stroud, listed the starting lineup for the Yellow Jacket team as follows: Left end # 83 Johnny Gray, Left tackle #74 Johnny Green, Left Guard #72 James Davis, Center #64 William Bentley, Right Guard #81 Robert Starling, Right Tackle #73 Curtis Carthon, Right End #84 Robert Smith, Quarterback #10 Bobby Sander, Left Halfback #22 Albert Wyche, Right Halfback #43 Charlie Carthon, and Fullback #82 Jesse Person. The Jackets dressed players in gold jerseys and black pants with black numerals and white helmets.

Drake High Sport Reporter Arthur Stroud stated, "After losing a well fought battle to Henry County Training School in McDonough, Ga. in the first game of the season, the Drake High Yellow Jackets journeyed to Barnesville, Georgia to sting the Booker High Tiger 19 to 6.

Yellow Jacket's Senior Quarterback Bobby Sanders returned the open kick-off for a touchdown and passes for another one. In the opening seconds, Sanders 71 yards touchdown gave the Jackets a 7-0 lead early in the game. In the second quarter eagle eyed Sanders connected with fullback Jesse Pearson on a 25 yard pass for a touchdown to give the jackets a 13-0 lead. In the third quarter Monroe "Jet" Banks cut loose for a spectacular 68 yard to insure the Jackets a hard fought 19 to 6 victory over Booker. The sparkling defense play was led by James Davis, Charles King, Jesse Pearson, and William Bentley.

In the season home opener the Yellow Jackets' Albert Wyche and Bobby Sanders returned intercepted passes to lead the Drake Hi Yellow Jacket to a 13 to 0 victory against Bobbie High of Milledgeville, Georgia in a Thursday night game at the old football field. In the second quarter Yellow Jacket's Albert Wyche, scored on 25 yard pass interception to give the Yellow Jacket a 6-0 lead. Before a large enthusiastic crowd in the attendance of the first home game, Bobby Sanders, in the fourth quarter intercepted a pass and ran 50 yards for Drake's final score to give the Jackets a 13 to 0 victory. The Yellow Jackets extended a two game winning streak.

In the third game of the season, Monroe "Sketter" Banks scored twice to help the Yellow Jackets fly pass the Hubbard High School Tigers of Forsyth, Georgia by a magnificent score of 25 to 6. In the first quarter, Banks ripped off a power-packed 15 yards touchdown to put the Jackets on the scoreboard 7-0. Later in the quarter, Big Jesses Pearson shattered the Tiger line for a 10 yard touchdown run to make the score 13-6. Late in the third quarter, Charlie Carthon scored on a 10 yards touchdown to push the score 19 to 6. Late in the fourth quarter, Monroe Banks showed his pass-catching ability. Eagle eyed Quarterback Bobby Sanders hit Banks with a 25 yard touchdown to give the hot Yellow Jackets a 25 to 6 victory. James Davis, Robert starling, Jesse Pearson, Monroe Banks, Bobby sanders, Charlie Carthon, William Bentley won praise from the coaching staff.

The first time in a decade or more, the Yellow Jackets were nearing a play-off and championship. The Drake High School Yellow Jackets invaded Fort Valley, Georgia for a game with the Hunt High Tigers that ended in a 20-20 tie. The Yellow Jackets were trailing 20 to 6 when on a turning point William Bentley intercepted a Tiger pass late in the third quarter. Big booming Jesse Pearson ripped the side line for a touchdown and Bobby Sanders added the extra point and the score was 20-13.

In the fourth quarter, Eagle Eye Bobby Sanders completed a series of passes before he found his favorite receiver, Johnny Gray, for a 25 yard touchdown and Jesse Person added the extra point to tie the game 20-20. Seniors, William Bentley and Monroe Banks of Drake were named to the High School All-Star Football Team. After the game William Bentley, a 3 year veteran commented "this is truly the finest team I have played with in the last two years." The cheer leaders, who were with the team through all kind of weather are Danny Smith, Mildred Stinson, Martha Weathers, Evelyn Walker, Mary Esther Pearson, Ruth Smith, and Gracie Reviere.

For the first time in 12 years, the "Yellow Jackets of Drake High, won the 1962 State Championship in Basketball. Drake High Sports Reporter, Arthur Stroud states, "This personifies the best in the state." Already the Jackets won second in District competition, then went on to go out front in the Simi-state tournament held at Drake High School to defeat teams from Louisville and Forest Park to qualify for a position in the state class "A" tournament, held in Swainsboro. The Jackets defeated Valdosta by a score of 66-47. Monroe Banks, James Wonunm, and Charlie Hobbs were credited in this victory for their all-around plays. The Jackets led all the way in this game, with James Wonunm probably playing the best game of his High School career, along with the spectacular offense and defense skills shown by Charles Hobbs. After winning this game, the Jackets had a determination to win the class "A" championship when they met East Depot High of LaGrange for the second time. The Jackets suffered a heart-breaking defeat at the hand of Depot on their home court, however, the Jackets sat back patiently and waited to meet them on neutral grounds. Even though Depot was good, they knew they were better.

The first quarter score was 21-11, led by the very offensive play of Monroe Banks and the rebounding of Curtis Carthon and Bobby Sanders. The Jackets were able to make over 60 percent of their shots and outplayed East Deport in every phase of the game. Again, the amazing "bottle neck" defense ability of James Wonunm paid off in dividends. The half score was 33-29. At this point, the Yellow Jackets had led all through the game and the tremendous fast break that were noted for the first time since the semifinal.

In the third quarter, the Jackets were sporting a 49-41 lead, but were confident the state championship was in reach. This was the quarter that spectators saw the great versatility possessed by the team. The Jackets put on a magnificent show of ball handling, rebounding (ball hawking), and the amazing "point" splurge that won the game. In the fourth quarter with an eight points, lead with eight minutes to play in the game, the Jackets out played Deport in every respect to make them victorious by the score of 69-53.

It can well be said, that this team has been one of the most exciting teams that Drake and Thomaston have seen in the last decade. Over a period of three years, Coach Eugene P. Walker's teams have compiled a record of 63 wins, against 8 defeats. This is an outstanding record and we can say without a doubt he is truly one of the state's most aggressive coaches, and a P.H.D. in basketball. The coach commented, "that the boys have played dedicated ball all year long, and the state semi-final was no exception".

The following seniors will leave one of the most distinguished records in basketball the Drake and Thomaston have seen. Seniors James Wonunm, Johnny Gray, Bobby Sander, and Curtis Carthon will be graduating this spring. The player's lefts to carry on next year are Charles King, Earnest Wilder, Monroe Banks, Charles Hobbs, and George Washington.

We could not single out any player as outstanding player for the season. The entire team should be commended for their exceptional display of of team dedication, spirit, sportsmanship, and versatility. The Jackets were helped to victories by loyal fans that was behind them in every game.

The Drake High State Champion Class A Basketball Team in its quest for national honors was successful in its first effort toward these honors. The cage men from Drake trounced a fast team from Folkston Friday Night, but they fell by the wayside Saturday night in Atlanta. Price High of the city defeated our boys by a rather large margin. The defeat, however, does not dim the luster of this well trained team. They are definitely the best in their class.

In December 1962, the Drake High School Gym was rocking as a large crowd witnessed a basketball game between Clark College and Fort Valley State College on a Monday night. Clark walloped Fort Valley by a lopsided score of 110 to 62. Two local boys were members of the college squad. Curtis Carthon was playing with Clark College and appeared briefly in both halves. Bobby Sanders was a member of the Fort Valley State College team and played for a short period during the first half.

Words of praise are due those persons who ventured the long ride to Statesboro to witness the Yellow Jackets repeat the 1963 Class A State championship over archrival, East Depot High School of LaGrange. A busload of students under the sponsorship of Miss Betty P. Williams, John Vaughn, and George Jennings made an outing of the affair, stopping in Dublin for lunch and several other places of interest. For many, this was their first trip to the eastern section of the state.

There were carloads of fans that made the trip. Many were still on the road trying to get back at daybreak. The team, its coach, and our principal, stated, "that they could not have fared better at a tournament, unless it was at home". Defending Class "A" state champion, Drake High School, brought an old antagonist to justice Saturday night at the William James High School Gym in Statesboro, Georgia.

East Depot Wolverines of La Grange, an annual emesis to the Jackets, received a sound 75-66 thrashing as standing room only crowd of screaming spectators seemed to have chosen sides cheered along with the Jacket fans. East Depot for the second straight year humiliated the Jackets by defeating them in District play-offs. Both teams cleared all obstacles in State semifinal each year to go to the finals. Both years these two teams played for the state championship crown and in both cases the Jacket brought the Wolverines hopes down in shambles.

The Jackets took the tip-off with beautiful play from Charlie Hobbs' tip to Tommy Chatman, who passed to James Wonunm who ended up in a whole tray of cups filled with soft drinks. The sight of cups and popcorn going up in the air and Wonunm going into the concessionaire was enough to dishearten the best. Time out was called while the floor was mopped and Wonunm and the concessionaire washed themselves off.

When play commenced again, the Jackets proved just too much for the Wolverines. Many had picked these teams to play in the finals, which came to be. The Jackets team justified its high ranking, for at one point in the second half, the Jackets romped to an 18 point lead. But fine performance by Wolverines' Willie Hall, Julius Hudson, and Calvin Simpson, reduced the gap to 3 points, which they could not maintain for more than one minute of play. Drake reporter, Dave Prather, reported that James Wonunm paced the win with 22 points, while Tommy Chatman hit 14, Charlie Hobbs added 11, Charles King, Monroe Banks, Willie Gene Atwater scored 8 points each. Earnest Wilder and Lewis Taylor also gave fine performances.

It just seemed that the Jackets could do no wrong. The Drake High School Yellow Jackets' 1963 State Championship Team consisted of Tony Chatman, Robert Starlin, James King, Willie Jean Atwater, Charlie Hobbs, James Wonunm, Earnest Wilder, Henry Wilder, and Monroe Bank. Co-caption and star member of the 1963 Drake Class A State Championship basketball team, Monroe Banks, was named to the South All-Star Basketball Team. Monroe left Tuesday morning for Atlanta where he will join the All-Star team for the All-Star classic, which will see the South against the North. The game will be played Wednesday night, July 31st at Washington High Gym

The Thomaston Times in October 1963 reported the City Officials met with the leaders of the Negro Community to propose to locate a pool adjacent to the Drake High School Gym. The officials offered to put $10,000 into the swimming pool and another $10,000 from Thomaston Mills that was pledged if the Negroes raised one-third the cost of their proposed $30,000 swimming pool by November 24 of the following year. The majority of the Negro leaders agreed in the presence of the City Official. But after the meeting most of the Negroes leaders wanted the lemonade, but did not want to squeeze the lemon. Chairman Monroe Worthy blamed a little bit of apathy as reason they did not want to measure up to expectations. He had faith that some were interested and would work. The women and educators of the Negro community began to plan and work hard to raise the funds. James C. Banks and H.D. Smith organized a salvage committee to pick up waste deposits next door to Green's Funeral Home on North Bethel Street... Co-chairwoman Julia C. Martin held a singing and baby contest at Macedonia Baptist Church. Rev. Marion Underwood, principal of Cunningham School, held programs at the school. Ora M. Kendall, teacher at Lincoln Park Elementary School, turned in donated checks. Britt Manufacturing donated $594.00. The new $30,000 Negro swimming pool was completed and dedicated in October 1964. The pool was located adjacent to the Drake High School and was operated by the school's physical education department during school months. The Drake Swimming Pool Committee consisted of Monroe Worthy, chairman, Julia E. Martin, vice-chairman, Elijah Worthy, Albert Walker, George I. Jennings, H.D. Smith, James C. Bank, Jr., Ollie Thurman, and A.S. Johnson.

The Negroes' history of Upson County accounted for some big stories that had a tremendous bearing on the civic, religious, and cultural behavior of our people. The year of 1964 saw the paving of most of the streets in Colored town. There was success in filling up some of our mud holes and at the same time eliminating a few dust bowls. One of the biggest stories of the year was the successful completion of the Drake High School Sports Complex. A Sports Complex with a metal and masonry building a gymnasium with dressing rooms, a basketball court, a football field and a new $30,000 swimming pool located adjacent to the gym were dedicated in October 1964. The port complex was operated by the school's physical education department during the school months.

The Thomaston Times edition in April 1965 the Drake High News reported, Rosa Marie Walton, a junior, was one of the 2,626 gifted high school students nominated for the Second Governor's Honor Program. Although Rosa was not among the final 400 selected to actually participate, she received a letter from Mrs. Margaret O. Bynum, Residential Administration, for the honors Program for having been nominated. Drake High School faculty and students were indeed happy to have such a student as Rosa in the midst.

The Thomaston Times edition in June 1965 reported, Under the leadership of *Mrs.* Mary A. Johnson, the wife of Principal Johnson, twenty-three Negroes students of the 1965 Drake High graduating class won scholarships for further schooling with a total value of over $8,000, and at least thirty of the forty six graduates were planning to seek higher education. The valedictorian, Marva Strickland, received an academic scholarship for $700 to attend Spelman College in Atlanta, Ga. The class salutatorian, Minder Rucker, received an academics and athletic scholarship to Morris Brown College in Atlanta, Ga., valued at $1985, for four years. Robert Kendall, Doris Furlow, Helen Atwater, Earnestine Walker, Edward White, Allene Woodard, and Geraldine Woodard each received grant-in-aide to Fort Valley State College in Fort Valley, Ga. Sandford Prater won a $400 athletic scholarship to Morris Brown. Three of the seniors- Patricia Hill, Allene Woodard, and Geraldine Woodard-received $100 scholarships each from the women's Federated Club. In addition, Vernice Kendall enrolled at Clark College and Tommie Lean Ivey enrolled at Fort Valley State College. David Harden, Willie James Walker, Billy Scott, Ora M. Townsend, Evelyn Walker, Jessie Mae Worthy, Patsy Moore, Flossie Monds, David Johnson, Herman Smith, and Mable Searcy enrolled in the vocational school. Two of the seniors, Marvin Ellerbee, and Andy Mallory took civil service jobs in Washington, D.C. and enrolled in night classes there. Principal Andrew Johnson commenting on the unusually high percentage of the 1965 class seeking higher education said that they already had high standards set for them by Drake Alumni already in college. More than fifty percent of our graduates in college are making the Dean's List.

The Drake High School Class of 1969 graduated the largest number of students in the history of the school. Superintendent G. R. Holstun presented a record number of 62 diplomas.

1967-69 Drake High School
Principal Andrew S. Johnson

Teacher	Degree Attained	School Attended
Raymond Adair	B. S. Agriculture	University of Georgia
Doris Curry	B.S. Library Science	Alabama State
Sgt. Thomas R. Dunn		U. S. Military
Betty Fergerson	B.S. Home Economic	Morris Brown
Daniel Hunter	B. S. English	Savanna State
Mary Johnson	B.S. Guidance Counselor	Clarke College
Joyce Lockhart	B.S. History	Fort Valley State
Deloris McIvey	B.S. Home Economic	Fort Valley State
James Townsend	B.S. Social Science	Fort Valley State
John Vaughn	B.S. Science	Morehouse
Robert Walls	B.S. Mathematics	Savannah State
Catherine Moore	B.S. Foreign Language	Fort Valley State
Gussie Flack	B.S. Visiting Teacher	Fort Valley State
T. C. Floyd	B.S. Mathematics	Alabama State
Edna Goodson	B.S. Business Education	Alabama State
Morris Patterson	B.S. History	Albany State
Dan Stilies	B.S. English	Georgia Southern

Dan Stiles, an instructor at Drake High, reported in *The Thomaston Times edition in February* 1968 *that the* Lady Yellow Jackets finished second in the Region and District Basketball Tournament in Roberta and Swainsboro. Swainsboro would host the State region tournament and the State finals of the G.I.A. Class A State Tournament would be held at the Drake High Gymnasium. For the season, the hustling Jackets had stopped 22 teams while dropping only four games. Two of their feats came during the regular season, while the other two were a result of the district and the region tournament in which they placed second in both encounters. In the battle for a state berth, the Yellow Jackets defeated Fairburn of Atlanta 59-53, in two overtimes with Mary Watson, a speedy, shifty forward hitting two pressure free throws to wrap up the victory. In the semi-finals, led by Watson's 30 points, the Drake sextet managed a 42-36 victory. In the final game, Pike County who defeated Drake girls twice before, remained consistent and gained 1st place honors, 45-40. Louise Randall, an eighth grader who led the Lady Jackets in scoring for the season and starting forward, suffered a broken leg and would not see action in the state tournament. The Drake Girls would play the team from Gray, Georgia in the second game on Friday. Other teams participating in the week end tournament were Tifton, Morgan, Madison, Springfield, Irvington, and Pike County. In the championship game, Pike County continued their donating and defeated the Lady Jackets for the fourth time to deny them the championship.

The Thomaston Times January 1970 edition stated the Drake High Yellow Jacket's Basketball Team had a winning effort from James Dixon and Milton Raines as Roberta fell to them in overtime, 70-67. The Yellow Jacket's James Dixon, was the heavy shooter for the winner, but his show was supercede by the efforts of Jimmy Barner, who sank 25 points to lead his team. Drake ripped off to a 15-8 lead in the first quarter. The Yellow Jackets, also dominated the boards. The Eagles of Roberta felt the loss of senior forward Allen Pagen as the Yellow Jacket dominated most of the first half. The best the Eagles could do was come within six points at the half, with Drake leading 32-26. The Eagles came out in the second half with a full court press defense, and behind Mitchell Blassigames' 9 points in the third quarter, but the Yellow Jackets still led 44-39. At the end of the 4th quarter the Yellow Jackets wasn't lucky after the Eagles tied the game on a turn over by sophomore guard, Charles Kendall. As a result of a lay-up by Eagles' Blassingame with 30 seconds to play forced the game into overtime. In a thriller the Drake High Yellows jackets out-lasted the Eagles in overtime by the score of 70-67. The Yellow Jackets were led by Senior, James Dixon, with 29 points and Milton Raines, with 19 points. Charles Kendall scored 9: Jerome Green scored 5; James McDaniel and John Harris scored 2 each and Elmo Seay also scored 1 point.

The Thomaston Times February 1970 edition reported Mrs. Mary Alice Johnson, the wife of Professor Andrew Johnson, passed at the Upson County Hospital after extended illness. Mrs. Johnson was employed by the board of Education for some sixteen or more years. First, as a teacher, at Lincoln Park Elementary, and later as a counselor for all the schools in the system. As a counselor, she was instrumental in getting scores of boys and girls scholarships to various colleges, which enabled them to continue their education after finishing high school which would not been possible without her help. The boys and girls owed Mrs. Johnson full measure of her efforts in helping them to get where they were.

In April 1970 the Drake's Drama Club presented a play at the annual District Three Dramatic Festival in LaGrange, Georgia entitled "The Refuge" that obtained a rating of excellent. For the spring attraction, the playmaker of Drake High School proudly presented a farce comedy in three acts entitled, "Grandad Steps Outs".

It was a wild and hilarious comedy about an old man who had been ill for a year. The old man was still considered an invalid by his daughter. The old man was fed nothing but soup and crackers, while he dreams of nothing but thick juicy steak. This play was held in May 1970 in the Drake high School Cafeteria. The comedy was directed by Miss Portia Elaine Wilson and Mr. Daniel D. Hunter.

The characters in the play were: Andrea Johnson, Gary King, Mary Childs, Dianne Kendall, Peggy Weathers, James McGill, Cleona Middlebrooks, Minnie Walker, Curtis Respress, Jerome Green, Valencia Walton, Carolyn Bush and James Johnson.

The Thomaston Times edition in September 1966 reported Drake High School had been approved by the Department of the Army for a junior ROTC unit and Supt. Gordon R. Holston announced it was activated for the 1967-68 school year. The military training taught patriotism, discipline, respect for those in command, neatness in dress, and gave a good underlying background in military training. It brought potential leadership to the top and provided the motivation for those with ambition to move ahead and amount to something.

In World War II, the Korean War, and in the Vietnam conflict, those who had junior R.O.T.C. training at R.E. Lee Institute found it of immeasurable value when they entered the armed Forces for active duty. This news from Supt. R. Holston of approval of the unit at Drake was met with pleasure by Negro and white communities who wished the best for all of the community's school children.

Colonel Robert J. Heckert, senior Army Instructor for Drake and R.E. Lee, announced David J. Searcy was commissioned a cadet major at Drake High and named the first and only battalion commander of the R.O.T.C. unit at the school. Colonel Heckert also announced other officer appointments, including Ben W. Respress as cadet captain, and second-ranking officer as executive officer. He named as first lieutenants on the battalion staff, Gary L. Green, Jerry Vinson, Melvin Kendall, and Willie J. Woodard. He commissioned Lt. James E. Thomas as Company A Commander, and Lt. Daniel Mann as Company B Commander. Other officers named were second lieutenants: Lt. Abner Ivey, Lt. Willie J. Walker, both battalion officers, and Lt. James R. Atwater, Lt. Alton Releford, Lt. Bobby V. Reeves, Lt. Jimmy Caldwell, Lt. Asmus L. Potts, Lt. Willie Childs and Lt. Albert Campbell all platoon leaders.

R. E. Lee High School in Thomaston, Georgia

INTEGRATION

The Thomaston Times edition in August 1965 reported Thomaston and Upson County School systems adopted a plan of desegregation to open a door to put cracks in a glass ceiling of all-white schools. The adoption of a policy of complete freedom of choice was offered annually in all grades of schools without regard to race, color, or national origin.

This choice was granted to parents, guardians, persons acting as parents. Teachers, principals, and other school personnel were not permitted to advise, recommend, or otherwise influence choices. They were not permitted to favor or penalize children because of choices.

Transportation was provided on an equal basis without segregation or other discrimination because of race, color, or national origin. The right to attend any school in the system was not restricted by transportation polices or practices. Teachers and staff desegregation were of school desegregation plan. Steps were taken beginning with school year 1665-66 toward elimination of segregation of teachers and staff personnel based on race, color, or nationality origin.

Seven Yatesville High students and thirteen R.E. Lee High students opened the door to put twenty cracks in a glass ceiling of white high schools. The thirteen Negroes students transferred to Robert E. Lee High School were: freshmen, Raymond Bentley, Bonnie Mallory, and Horace Atwater; sophomores Mary Fagan and Larry Prater; juniors Lawrence Davis, Jacquelyn Fagan, and Camille Smith; and seniors John Carter, Robert E. Prater, and Andrew Stinson. The seniors, Carter, Prater and Stinson, were the first Negroes to receive high school diplomas from Robert E. Lee Institution.

In 1968, Principal, Solomon Johnson, decided not to have a football team at Drake High School. The Negro students were told by the coaches at R.E. Lee High School that there was no place for boys from Drake

High School to play in the program. The school carried out an organized effort to make sure that these players would not fit in the program. This challenge opened doors for the former Drake players to put cracks in the glass ceiling in the sports world at the school. Mitchel Carthon put a crack in a glass ceiling by being awarded first letter on R.E. Lee Rebel Football team. Carthon drew a pat on the back from Lee Coach Jim Cavan when he was presented a Rebel Jacket at the annual banquet. Coach Cavan said, "This is the first time a colored boy ever received an L, at Lee. Mitchel is a gentleman on and off the field and he was a complete boy. He should be proud of the things he accomplished at Lee." When the Lee end stepped forward to receive his jacket he drew a round of applause from his teammates and coaches. Mitchel went on to graduate from Savanna State College and worked his way up to a Major in the U.S. Marine Corp.

Henry Childs also put a crack in a glass ceiling by being awarded the first Negro to receive a letter on the R. E. Lee boys' basketball team under Coach Wallace Rhodes. Henry went on to graduate from the University of Georgia, and to become Captain in the U.S. Army. He was one of the first Negro to fly an airplane while serving in the Army.

Dorothy "Pat" Ellerbe also put a crack in a glass ceiling by being awarded the first letter on the lady Rebels basketball team under the late Coach Jim Cavan. Dorothy went on to graduate from Spelman College and returned to Thomaston to join the staff as a P.E. Teacher on the campus of R.E. Lee high School. After many years of striving, she became the first, and only lady of color to be the head coach for the high school girls' team since integration.

Raymond Bentley became the first Negro to be awarded a letter for the rebel baseball team from Coach Tommy Perdue. Bobby Drake put a crack in a glass ceiling by being the first black to lead a R. E. Lee platoon drill team in competition with teams from five states. Drake won the outstanding drill of manual of arms.

The Historic Upson County Negro School System served the Negro Community for exactly 100 years (1870-1970). The 107th Anniversary of Emancipation Proclamation Celebration of the May 29, 1970 was the last official time the faculty and students of this school system would be recognized without knowing it at the time.

The high stepping Drake High Yellow Jacket Marching band, along with the Booker High School Band from Barnesville, led the parade of the107ᵗʰ Anniversary of Emancipation Proclamation Celebration of the May 29, 1970, down Bethel Street and through downtown into Lincoln Park for a program. The Rev. C. H. Atwater served as master of ceremonies at the Lincoln Park site of the Emancipation Proclamation program. Earnest Ferguson, president of the event, presented the greeting remarks from Emancipation Association. Rev. A. Willis was the devotional leader while Rev. F. R. Strickland was in charge of the Scripture. Rev. C. R. Johnson gave the invocation while music was furnished by the Drake High School Band. Miss Toni Saleeta, sixth grade student gave the welcoming address. James Franko, Monroe G. Worthy School principal, appeared on the program along with Arlie Zorn, past president of the association.

The Booker High School Band appeared on the program with music for the huge crowd in Lincoln Park. Also appearing on the program were Rev. R. H. Martin, presiding elder of the Milledgeville District of the AME Church; J. E. Bentley of Bentley's and Son Funeral Home; Mrs. J. E. Martin, Supervisor of the Upson County Negro School System, Andrew S. Johnson, Drake High School principal and retired principal of Monroe G. Worthy School.

Rev. Minor Rucker recognized the visitors while Faye White read the Emancipation Proclamation. Rev. L. C. Culbreast, pastor of Friendship Baptist Church in Lincoln Park introduced Rev. C. J. Johnson, pastor, evangelist, and recording artist from Atlanta, Georgia as the guest speaker.

The Thomaston Times in August 1970 reported that the Thomaston Board of Education responded to a federal mandate to integrate its public school system by closing all-Negro schools. This was forcing southern schools to become compliant to the Supreme Court ruling in 1954 Brown versus Board of Education some 16 years later.

That erupted into a deep entrenched legalized segregation in the county. Dependent upon federal funds to keep local schools afloat, local school systems in the former slave belt were forced to find ways to implement integration. Their approaches were clearly designed to lessen fear and resentment among white citizens.

In general, the Thomaston Board of Education was insensitive to the feelings of African Americans. The movement and the federal government agreed that integration was the propitious way to provide quality educational opportunities for all children. Three years after the assassination of Dr. Martin Luther King, Jr., the civil rights movement was all but dead but its legacy lived on.

The Thomaston Times edition in August 1970 reported, Drake High and Elementary School was closing and all eighth graders were transferred to the East Thomaston Elementary School and students and faculty from Drake Elementary were distributed among the three remaining city grammar schools. Drake High School students went to Robert E. Lee High School, which remained as a four-grade school.

City School Supt. Harold Maguire said in his announcement "that the changes were made in order to comply with requirements as outlined by the Department of Health, Education, and Welfare, and order to continue efforts to provide the best educational opportunities for all the children of Thomaston. This plan was in the process of implementation over the past several years. Since, this same step was one of the recommendations made by a representative committee of Negro citizens (Mrs. Leatha McMullin, Mr. J.E. Bentley, and Rev. R.R. Smith, Chairman) in September of last year, the City Board of Education felt that this decision was in accord with the wishes of a majority of the Negro citizens of Thomaston."

The closing of Drake eliminated all predominately-Negro schools in the city school system. The majority of Negro communities were not very happy. A group of community leader called a meeting one August night at the Teen Age Center on the Park Street Playground. These Community Leaders invited the Drake High School students to the meeting.

The Community Leaders gave the students directive to go in the street to march until they go to jail. The Negro Community Leaders would come and get them out of the jail. The Negro Community Leaders thought it was very important for the students to go to jail to save their school. All the students agreed to carry out their wishes to go to jail trusting the leaders to get out of jail.

Early the next morning most of the Negro students gathered on the Drake High School Campus doing negative things in order to go to jail. Sending rags up the flag pole and talking rudely to the Thomaston Polices Department, as they watch the activities. The student's sang Negro

Spirituals all day long, the Thomaston Polices Department watched as nothing more happened.

Finally, the students asked permission to march to the Park Street Playground. The students marched toward the playground, and one of the students cried out "lets march through the heart of town." As the students passed Walker Street and about to cross the railroad track, the Thomaston Polices Department came in from all over the city to block them from marching beyond the railroad track.

The Thomaston Polices Department ordered the marchers to turn back and go to the playground. Remembering the white reporter's interview with Mrs. Blakely a former slave, which said that "before a slave could leave the district it was necessary to obtain a pass. If a slave was caught out without a pass, there were men known as Patrollers' who appointed themselves, to punish the slaves."

At that point, the students retreated back to the playground. A portion of the group wanted a permit to march. One girl, and twenty-five boys, left the playground marching to City Hall. The Thomaston Police Department Chief led the students down stairs and locked them up. News spread of the students arrest at City Hall. Students from all over the county came to join the protest by demanding to be arrested also. By night, the number was up to about 70 negro students locked in jail. The Community Leaders, as planned, arrived at the City Hall to get the students released from the city jail to their parents.

On the following Tuesday Night, August 18, 1970, a petition was submitted to the Thomaston Board of Education by some Negro Community Leaders consisting of Mr. Monroe Worthy (Chairman), Mr. J.E. Bentley Jr., Mrs. Gertrude Harper, Mrs. Carolyn McGill- Holmes, Mr. Eugene Walker, and Mr. Jerry Walker Sr.

This petition stated that with the closing of Drake High school, there was an awakening and a frustrating sense of an extension of a past mistreatment we wish not to forget.

Our hope of a tranquil, joyous co-existence died of self-suffocation. This was a firm resolution that we cannot smile at the opening of school. The Negro community was experiencing the painful pregnancy of our struggle. We know we must challenge you in a concrete, absolute manner in order to survive as a race and maintain our dignity. This is the first time in the history of Thomaston that all Negroes have assembled their talents to devise a methodology toward gaining unity and working together for our self-respect.

We have worked arduously since the closing of Drake diagnosing our problems and theorizing solutions. We dealt with a number of topics, namely, educational, integration, and curriculum development. We are obligated at this point, to share with you some of our conclusions regarding the aforementioned topics.

On the subject of education, the Negro Community feels that the affective aspect of knowledge should be given the same consideration as the cognitive aspect. To thrust our Negro students into a previously all white setting to acquire knowledge without considering their feelings and attitudes, while placing no white students in a previously all black setting is psychologically unsound. We, the Negro Citizens of Thomaston, cannot sit idly by and allow this to happen.

We are not fighting integration, for we feel that it is desirable in some instance and essential in the world of work as well as in the future development to this country. However, we want to integrate with dignity to maintain our self-respect, and to preserve our race. Integration short of these goals is very undesirable and resisted until our last breath.

We also conclude that the curriculum must include subjects on Negro History and life style, emphasizing our African Heritage. This is essential in the education of our Negro youth. These convictions have been expressed with the feeling that you will not re-open Drake and establish a biracial committee for a number of reasons, among which are the facts that time is of essence and the county has already taken over the school building and made plans for its use.

However, there are a number of things that can be done to insure the cooperation of Negroes in carrying out your edict. However, before listing our demands we would like everyone to know that we do not condone the efficacy of riots, demonstrations, and economic boycotts if there is any possible way for them to be averted. We do believe, however, that when responsible leaders of any race come together in good faith with respect for each other and intent on being fair, a tolerable solution is forthcoming. It is this latter premise that we pray will prevail as we attempt to gain our manhood and exercise our citizenship.

The Thomaston Times edition in August 1970 reported a listing of the Negro Community Leaders demands and The Thomaston Board of Education an answers. The Negro Community Leaders filed and requested that the Superintendent and Board of Education should:

1. Establish a biracial committee to discuss ways and means of bridging gap between black and white students.
   - Answer: There was a mutual agreement that a biracial committee would be valuable as a mean of bridge the gap between black and white students, and recommended from such a committee would be assistance to the Board it its deliberation points. It is also felt that there would probably be two committees: one which would be composed of responsible adults within the committee; one which would be composed of responsible students within the high school. Suggestions for arriving at membership on this committee;.
   - Adult- committee of eight-four members to be selected by the Negro committee presenting the petition, and four members selected by the Board of Education. (No member of the Board of Education was to serve on the committee)
   - Student committee of twenty – ten members selected by the respective Student Councils to be advised by both a Negro and a white faculty member.
2. Keep Robert E. Lee and Drake High School open and place some white students in Drake High and some Black students in Robert E. Lee.
   - In view of the immediacy of the opening of school the position of the Department of Health and Education and Welfare that no further delays will be allowed in the implementation of the plan s which were approved, the fact that the County System has already taken over and arranged for their use of the building formally housing Drake High school, and the plans, moving, and arrangements which was already take place the decision was the plans as announced. The superintendent and the Board of Education earnestly solicit the cooperation of all citizens of Thomaston in making this program successful.

3. If the two high schools are not continued in use, change the name of the school from Robert E. Lee to Thomaston High School.
   - Answer to Question #3, 4, 10, and 11
     - These points would appear to more directly relate themselves to further study by one or both of the biracial committees as the board would seek their recommendations in attempting to arrive at successful long-term solution.
4. Fill the next five (5) vacancies on the school board with Negroes.
5. Hire a Negro Counselor that Negro students can relate to and can aid them in adjusting to this new situation.
   - The hiring of a qualified, and certified, Negro Counselor is under consideration at the present time. A Negro Counselor from the County System was cooperatively involved in the re-scheduling of students for the year. Such a position would be filled as practical, not to relate to just Negro students, but to complement the total educational program. The Negro teachers within the various schools also provide valuable assistance as adjustments are made.
6. The use of symbol and participation in activities, which are, affronts to minority group (white or black), e.g. the singing or playing of "Dixie" flying Confederate flag should be prohibited.
   - The Board and Superintendent does take the position that all symbols and activities should be eliminated which are real and significant affronts to a representative group of students, black and white, and will inform school principals. This point could also relate itself to the student committees.
7. Clubs and organizations which existed at the previous schools under segregation should be allowed and encouraged to reorganize in the desegregated schools on a nondiscriminatory basis.
   - All club and organization which existed at the previous school; and which make a significant contribution to the educational program of the institution, will be encourage continuing on nondiscriminatory basis and without specific racial identification.
8. Medals, plaques, trophies, pictures, certificates, which are normally displayed by schools should be transferred to and displayed by the

receiving school, in keeping with the traditional policy as practiced in the past.

9.

- Medals, plaques, trophies, certificates, normally displayed by schools will be transferred to and displayed by the receiving school as space comes available; a fair selective process may have to be followed for the immediate future.

10. No school-connected activity should be held at a place where racial discrimination is practiced.

- It is the present policy that no school sponsored activity is held at a location where members of both races cannot attend.

11. New symbols of identification including school song, mascot, yearbook, newspaper, school color, etc.

12. Procedures for election to and qualification for leadership roles such as cheerleaders, majorettes, athletic team captains, class and club officers, school representatives (Homecoming Queen, Sweethearts, Student Government representative, and officers, etc.)

13. Classroom teachers in the system should be employed in direct racial proportion to the racial composition of the student population within the system.

- Classroom teachers are employed in relation to system needs, and individual certification and qualification. It is anticipated that the racial composition of the student population will be an important consideration in the selection of teachers for the system, but it is also felt that to follow a specific percentage ratio would not necessarily work to the advantage of the students or the system.
- Mr. H.O Maguire, Superintendent, and member of the Thomaston Board of Education stated "the decision to close Drake High School was reached after much serious deliberation and careful consideration of all facets of our local situation. There is keen awareness that groups and individuals of both races will face problems and difficulties for which solutions must found. It is the sincere feeling of the Board and the Superintendent that all citizens of Thomaston, working

in harmony on a mutual problem, will find successful and satisfactory solutions of these difficulties.

- A planned program, approved by the Department of Health, Education, and Welfare, has been in the process of implementation over the past several years to bring about a unified school system for Thomaston. This final step was one of the recommendations made by a representative committee of Negro citizens (Mrs. Leatha McMullin, Mr. J.E. Bentley, Jr., Rev. R. Smith, and Chairman). It was felt that this decision was in accord with the wishes of a majority of the Negro citizens of Thomaston.

- It is the desire of the Board and Superintendent to provide the best educational opportunities possible for all students in Thomaston, and it is our earnest conviction that under this plan were more able to provide for these opportunities. Some of the principal advantages resulting from the implement of this plan will be the provision for smaller class sizes an opportunity for ability grouping, resulting in more individual attention for students the possibilities of needed special programs of study through the more effective use of total faculty as the obvious financial advantage accruing through this operation."

- A petition by the Alumnae of Robert E. Lee Institution and/ or interested Citizens of Thomaston and Upson County, Georgia on behalf of the same for maintaining the name and tradition of Robert E. Lee Institution presented a petition to The Thomaston Board of Education. For grounds therefore, petition show: The Robert Lee Institution was charted in 1875. For the past ninety-five (95) years this school has served Thomaston and Upson County in the grandest of academic traditions. It was named for one of the most learned and gentlest of Southern Gentlemen. On its hallowed wall hangs the portrait of one of this nation's most renowned military geniuses-General Stonewall Jackson. Will you pull this down? Robert E. Lee Institution is steeped in southern academic traditions. To change the name of this institution would be an affront to the many thousands of alumnae and graduates, both past and present, who proudly reflect their sojourn in the hallowed halls of this one's superb academy of learning. That, we, your petitioners pray to you honorable members of this Board not to bend to the unreasonable demands of a small militant minority and erase our past tradition, and heroes.

- On October 15, 1970 the Thomaston Board of Education released the confirmation of appointment to an eight-member biracial committee who primary purpose is to study the petitions presented to the Board of Education earlier and to make recommendation to the Board. Member of the committee include Randall Drummond, S. W. Hempstead, Rev, Edwin L. Cliburn, Bobby Smith, Monroe Worthy, J.E. Bentley, Willie B. Harris and Joe Louise White. The committee was informed that its primary purpose was to study certain petition which had been presented to the Board of Education and to make recommendations regarding them.

- An organization meeting was held was held on Tuesday night, October 20, 1970, Rev. Edwin L. Cliburn was elected chairman; Mr. Monroe Worthy was elected Secretary. Underlying the thought and action of the committee was a desire to maintain a climate conducive to the continuing education of the children of our community. The committee agreed to work in an atmosphere of complete freedom of exchange and mutual respect. The recommendations presented to the Thomaston Board of Education were:

I.   The name R.E. Lee Institute was a name which has been borne by this school for many years. It is recognized that the man, R.E. Lee, was far more than a soldier of the confederacy. He was also a humanitarian and educator. At the same time it must be recognized that the Negro students lost a wholesome contact with their past and a helpful contact with their present community with the closing of Drake High School which had been named for Mr. George W. Drake of Thomaston.

- That the name R.E. Lee Institute be maintained.

- That the annex Building be named for Mr. George W. Drake with an appropriate a plaque being placed in the building honoring Mr. Drake. The plague should include appropriate reference to the school which bore his name for a number of years.

II. Different requirements for selecting majorettes were followed in R.E. Lee and Drake High School. When the schools were integrated the Drake majorettes were automatically excluded because of their inability to play musical instrument in the band. To reconcile this situation it is recommended:
- That requirements 1 and 2 used at R. E. Lee in the section of majorettes (this requirement call be waived for former Drake majorettes for the 1971-72 school year only.
- That requirement 3 remain in force

III. The position of Cheerleader was obtained through a competitive process. The committee realized that only qualified students should be allowed to serve. In this connection it was recommended:
- That all cheerleader requirements remain in force.
- That the selection group which chooses cheerleaders be reminded that a large segment of the student body is black and therefore Negro student (s) should be considered as a means of enhancing school spirit.
- That the administration of the school make a special effort to be sure that all students are informed as to training and tryout for this position.

IV. Inasmuch as the student council is to represent students in school affairs this body should have members from both races. To insure adequate and fair representation of both races on this body and in its executive committee it was recommended;
- That the present policy of election of homeroom representatives be continued.
- That the present policy of allowing any students interested in becoming a member of the student council to apply to its executive committee for membership at large be continued.

- That, if necessary, the executive committee be authorized to elect a number of members at large to carry out the sprit and purpose of this recommendation.
- That all members at large have voting privileges.

V. If the American Negro was to be seen in proper perspective as a part of contemporary American society, it is most important to know something of his origins and peculiar set of circumstances. In view of this your committee recommends:
- That a course in Negro History be offered to students at R.E. Lee High School with an effort to strengthen the contributions that Negroes made to Western Civilization.
- That the course be elective and made full credit be given.

VI. In matter relating to the Thomaston Board of Education the committee would make the following observations and then on the basis of their observations make two recommendations. We fell that the time will give both the Board of Education and the citizens of the community a better perspective of the more precise adjustments which might need to be made regarding the Board of Education itself. We feel that drastic changes at this time, either in the composition of the board of Education or the method of their celebration would not be the best interests of all concerned. It must be realized that students of both races are being called upon to make adjustments. Further changes at this time could easily create conditions which would detract from the opportunity of all students to have a wholesome climate for learning. It must not forget that the basic mission of the schools was to teach. In view of these observations, we would make these recommendations:
- We recommend that in view of the changes which have already been made in the school system, that serious future consideration should be given relative to the selection of the members of the Board of Education so as to broaden the representation of the citizens so that all areas of the entire community can be more adequately represented.

- We recommended that the Board of Education should make provisions to continue utilizing a representative bi-racial group as an advisory committee.

VII. Medal, plaques, and trophies, pictures, certificates, etc. are always valued by students and alumni of school. It was recognized that these emblems provide for a sense of loyalty and continuity of heritage. Therefore we recommend:
- That available class pictures from both R.E. Lee and Drake, by appropriately preserved and kept available for viewing. (One method of carrying out the spirit of this recommendation would be to bind these pictures into book from and keep them among the reserved books of the library.)
- That display cases be provided in appropriate locations for the display of all significant trophies of both Drake and R.E. Lee.

Conclusion:

It will be noticed that several matters mentioned in the various petition are not touched on the report. Some of these items are cared for under the regulations of the department of Health, Education, and Welfare, and some have already been handledl by local school officials, still others need to be delayed until the student by-racial committee has had an opportunity to meet and enter into discussions.

In a letter to the Biracial Committee and the Board of Education by a group of white citizens stated, "For many years now, Federal Government has subjected the southland to heavy pressures to abandon the biracial social structure. For many years the South has endured pressure, pushing desegregation, and added expense to satisfy the government and the Black power structures of the United States of American. It appears the more giving that is done, the more and more we will have to give in. It has been announced by Federal employees that education is of no importance to them; their goal is to achieve social reform. It appears that through the different organizations, representing the black People and through monies raised by these Black organizations, they have made substantial progress.

There have been laws changed and laws made just to fit the occasion, taking no consideration for the hurt or even the inconvenience that might be placed upon any other race of people. We, as Christians and open mined people, would go to any extent to honestly and educationally group or governmental power move in to purposely cram an unwanted situation; such as to socialize with anyone matter not who or what they might be— Then nothing but weak mined citizens would accept this as his plot in life.

There was a boundary placed during the time of our Lord. He walked among men of this land, preaching and leading people in the direction He would have them to go. There as a great separation during the time of Babel. There was a great separation during the time of Babel. There will always be a separation of the majority side. We realize that all Christians are indeed Brothers in Christ. In Christ there is no East or West, but Christian Brotherhood implies no sort of Equality beyond this and it certainly sets up no preemptive right of intrusion. Brothers are not equal and cannot be. Brotherhood is a status in a family. There are big brothers and little brothers; each with duties of his own and responsibility to the other. Christianity does not destroy the difference in men, it does something greater it makes those differences irrelevant.

So, Gentlemen, You see, no matter what direction you go if you pursue what the government officials really want, it can be justified in our way of thinking.

Certainly we have no gripes about our money and our intelligence coming to the aid of those less fortunate, but putting our inheritance on the chop block is stepping too far out of boundary. No matter how long we may sleep, when we awake we are still denying our heritage. From all the blood that flowed of great men who were trying to protect what had been there; for us to turn our backs or to brainwash ourselves and ignore the real facts of this city and country would be disgraceful and sinful to the greatest extent. Never should we forget the grand ole flag of Dixie and when Dixie is played we should Throw our shoulders back and stand at attention with pride. There are many things that we did not do to be a person with great name, but the many little things done by we little people caused the big things to happen. My father did not own and run a textile mill, but he grew some of the cotton that caused the mill to operate.

There are many circumstances we could quote to try and reason with our opposite color and ultimately try to reach a better understanding, but all the quotes and remarks that have been made by greater people has been to no avail.

Gentlemen, we have been the silent majority in Thomaston and Upson County since the big change in government, but thanks to our Lord, some several thousand of us have shaken ourselves and are ready to be heard through this organization as to our desires. We cannot and will not set idly by and watch our names be changed in any way shape or form. There are no ways or committees that can bridge the gap that God himself created; neither do we have any desire for a committee to try. As you can see it is an all we demand this or we demand that situation.

Why should five Negroes be placed on the school board? The Negroes and the federal Government themselves admitted they would have come to the white people for quality education, therefore, they are saying we want equal education in the class rooms but unequal representation on the boards. We feel this is nonsense and should be treated and passed on as such. We are not in favor of hiring any additional staff to further cause our wages and income to be taxed. Those people are being sent to our facilities by their own demands through the federal government.

We feel, as we have said earlier in this letter, the more you give the more you will have to give until eventually we along with the negroes will have nothing to give or anything to demand. The people of Thomaston and Upson County have had no voice in selection a biracial committee. Let us be understood when we say before any decisions from any group o organization is made final that will affect our children's children and so down the family tree. The entire city and county will have the privilege of voting. One of our pledges in this organization is that we will support whole heartedly our school board as long as they support the majority of the people of this city and county. This organization will help in any way we can to be service to the people. May God guide and direct you in your action." Sincerely, B. Fred Coggins (Chairman), M.K. Watson (Yatesville), Mrs. M.S. Black (Gordon), Henry O. Bell (Gordon), Ronald E. Salter (Atwater), Jimmy Harrell (Yatesville), Bobby Edmondson (Rock Hill), Williams D. Rogers (Thurston), and P.R. Maxwell (City)

In a letter from Thomaston Board of Education Superintendent Harold O. Maguire on February 15, 1971, to Rev. Edwin L. Cliburn, Chairman of the adult By-Racial committee, stated, "As a matter of information, the following action was taken by the Thomaston Board of Education relative to the recommendations recently submitted by the Adult Bi-Racial Committee:

I. That the name of R.E. Lee Institute is maintained, and the Annex Building be named for Mr. George W. Drake with an appropriate plaque being placed on the building—Approved. A committee to be established by the board to plan for the naming of the building and for an appropriate plaque.

II. Requirements for selection of Majorettes—Approved in principle and referred to the proper officials in the high school.

III. Qualifications for selection of Cheerleaders- Approved in principle and referred to proper officials in the high school to recommend beset method of implementation.

IV. Selection of members of the Student Council—Approval in principle and referred to the proper officials in the high school.

V. To established a course in Negro History—Approval in principle and referred to proper officials in the high school to recommend best method of implementation.

VI. Future makeup of the board of Education and continued utilization of a bi-racial advisory committee—The Board will take due cognizance of these recommendations in planning for the future.

VII. That medals, plaques, trophies, pictures and certificates be property displayed and preserved—all medals, plaques, and trophies are already in trophy cases at the high school. Certificates and pictures will be handled through the library for preservation and viewing.

In a statement on a local radio station the Negro students felt that after the closing of Drake High School they were thrown under the bus. The students felt that they had a better opportunity to express themselves at Drake. The students felt that at Drake, everybody seemed to be happy because they studied and played together with school spirit.

The entire school competed against other schools. There was no prejudice among schoolmates. At Lee, the white students out-number the black students; therefore, the black students were not elected to any offices. At Lee, the black students had any fun because the students felt as though the black student were trapped in a prison camp with no way out. The black students felt they were not given same opportunity as white students. It was a disgrace to have a black student on the student council.

In the Lee band, the majorettes had to be in the band at least two years and be able to play at least two instruments to be qualified. The black student could not meet this high qualification because they had been in the school for but one year. The cheerleaders had to attend summer camp for two years in order to be a cheerleader and continue to go every summer. Most black parent of the students could not afford to send their children.

The football team would only select one black student per season to participate. The black students felt the rules were separate for black and white students. The black students felt if they expressed their feelings to the teacher it was perceived as being disrespectful. Most of the teachers treated the black students as though they were inferior.

The white students attended and enjoyed the football and basketball games but the black student would probably get called into the office the next day to be accused of causing a disturbance. There were no black faculties in a position to positively support black students. The black students felt the name of the school should be changed because this was a combination between what was Drake and then Lee. The black students felt Drake had an equal tradition that fell on deaf ears. Since the Thomaston Board of Education had taken away a whole school, you would think that they would agree to combine the name of both schools.

History is an important part of our lives, and I hope that this book has allowed readers to look back into the past and remember those strong community leaders who shaped the foundation of our community.

Printed in the United States
By Bookmasters